Wealth for Life

The Business Owner's 9-Step Guide To Creating Wealth For Family & Life

Ben Walker

Client Endorsements

"I've been a client of Ben and the team at Inspire for five of the biggest 'rollercoaster' years I've ever had in business. Through starting multiple companies, dealing with COVID impacts, and helping me activate numerous investment decisions, their genuine interest in my overall 'family group' accounting and financial welfare has been a key to our success. His trusted network of referral specialists are now also my go-to. This is a must-read book for families setting out to build 'wealth for life'."

Michael P

"I've had the delight of working with Ben and his team over the past four years. I have come to see them as highly trusted partners. When I stepped out of a big corporate and started my own advisory business, Ben and the team were on hand to advise me on the best way to structure and manage my financials. When my father stepped down from managing our family super fund, Inspire respectfully and seamlessly stepped in to support us in the transition and ongoing management of the fund. When I've considered different types of 'wealth for life' investments, I've learned much from Ben and his team, and have valued their knowledge and insights in the decision-making process. I am certainly feeling as though we have the firm foundations, growth strategies, and the right structures to enable and protect our futures, from the 19 year old through to the 94 year old in my family."

Elisa H

"One of the best decisions I have ever made in business and life was to attend a workshop run by Inspire. Not only did it open my eyes to what I needed to change within my business, but it armed me with all the tools to do so. Having Ben and the team in my corner is like having a secret weapon; almost an unfair advantage. Ben and the team go above and beyond their role as our accountants and it is thanks to them we have the structure, the vision, and the confidence to create the intergenerational wealth I have always dreamt of for my family. Not only has Ben and the team helped me secure property with an amazing SMSF strategy, they guided me through the COVID period with business grant and eligibility advice. This is as well as helping with the everyday headaches when accounting hasn't been my forte. Ben and the team are always a call or a text away. I'm extremely lucky to have them in my corner and I encourage everyone to do the same!"

Steve W

"Ben has been our accountant and a trusted business adviser for my group of companies for around 8 years. His unwavering commitment, together with his amazing Inspire team, have assisted our business in a broad range of areas, including cash flow, tax, structures and some international tax matters. What makes Ben unique and awesome is his genuine passion for my business success and his ability to advise on generating family wealth. I am excited for the results that readers of Wealth For Life will have. It will give you the potential to achieve more, simply by investing the time to read, absorb and implement the principles Ben shares."

Steve C

Disclaimer

All the information, techniques, skills and concepts contained within this publication are of the nature of general comment only and are not in any way recommended as individual advice. The intent is to offer a variety of information to provide a wider range of choices now and in the future, recognising that we all have widely diverse circumstances and viewpoints. Should any reader choose to make use of the information herein, this is their decision, and the author and publisher(s) do not assume any responsibilities whatsoever under any conditions or circumstances. The author does not take responsibility for the business, financial, personal or other success, results or fulfilment of the readers' decision to use this information. It is recommended that the reader obtain their own independent advice.

Dedicated to my beautiful family – Stevie, Rose,
Ezra & Poppy.

Always remember: we all have the power to create a life
(and business) that gives us the ability to put
our family first.

Table of Contents

Table of Contents

Table of Contents

.

Introduction

Most business owners pour their heart into their business. They provide immense value to the community and business world, but they often don't get rewarded well until they work the kinks out of their business, which can take years, decades, or a lifetime to master. The result is that a lot of business owners struggle financially and take huge financial risks.

I do not want to see business owners struggle to get by as the norm. Or be better off in a job. Or get to the end of their business journey and have taken very little profit off the table to enjoy life along the way and grow their family wealth. If you follow the guidance in this book, it will change the trajectory you and your family are on, and hopefully, you'll end up in a place that you never even dreamt of!

I wrote this book primarily because I had so many challenges throughout my own wealth creation journey and I want to help other business owners avoid them, where possible. The problem was that I was in the first few years of running my business. Additionally, I did it without any personal financial backing and quickly got into a serious amount of debt after a few less-than-ideal business decisions.

For so many years, wealth creation seemed off the cards. I was focused on putting food on the table, paying the next BAS, making the next payroll date, and managing that huge debt. Over the years, my focus was to increase the cash generated from my business, pay down some debt, and *then* worry about building wealth. What I wanted to make sure of was that I didn't work the next few decades of my life, take on big risks, work big hours, and not have much to show for it at the end.

Business is hard enough, and there are not many people who will teach and show you how to create wealth, but I believe it is so important to build wealth outside of your own business. It can also be extremely confusing if you are new to investing and wealth creation concepts and have no idea who to trust.

There are a number of mistakes I have also seen myself or other clients make in the journey: things like trying to time the market, being too afraid to invest, overthinking it, overcomplicating it, being scammed, investing but expecting quick results, and plenty more. And the truth is there's no one way to do it. You'll probably make mistakes and lose money sometimes and, if you learn from them, you'll make some good decisions and end up being better off for it.

I wrote this book to share my experiences, but also to help you with different problems that I've faced personally around growing wealth, including how the concepts in this book can have a huge impact on your relationship with your spouse and the life you live with your family. For me, a pretty low point in life, and what caused me to make some change in my and my wife's wealth creation journey, was when my wife and I were on our honeymoon.

I was about two years into starting my accounting firm called Inspire, and my wife Stevie was in the final year of her veterinary science degree which consisted of full-time (unpaid) practical work for most of it, along with some crazy exams that she needed to study another 10+ hours for in the same week.

To introduce Stevie, here's a photo of us in Eli Creek on one of our early trips to Fraser Island. Why we picked that year to get married, I still don't quite know!

Given what we were each doing professionally, neither of us had much time for each other. Neither of us had much money at all either, with Stevie not working and Inspire not generating much of a return (in fact, it was going backwards at times). We were in a state where we lacked direction as a couple. We couldn't see our way out of the crap financial situation we were in, and we needed to do something about it.

So, we packed our bags and headed two hours west of Brisbane, to a retreat called Spicers. We stayed there for two nights. The afternoon arrived, and we spent it doing the exercise that I suggest in part one of this book: mapping out our personal Bucket Lists. This step alone got us started on a journey together as a couple, planning out our goals and dreams. What was quite surprising is over the coming five to seven years, we started ticking off a lot of the goals that we had set.

It started with relatively easy goals, but as time passed and we came closer to the time when we hoped to tick off our bigger goals, our dreams then started to turn into reality: such as travelling to plenty of countries (after both not travelling much in our lives at all), starting a family together, as well as buying our dream home, our first investment property and a holiday apartment. Reflecting back to that moment at Spicers is a bit surreal, as it makes me think about how far we've come together as a couple since then.

My hope for you in reading this book is that it might be your 'Spicers moment', if you are beginning your journey or if you want to speed up your journey. Hopefully, you're not in the exact situation that we were in, with a serious lack of time and money, but rather at the start of a 5-to-7-year journey where you completely transform where you are and where you are heading, from a relationship, family, and financial perspective.

What This Book Will Share

This book will teach you the 9 steps I've put together to create wealth for life. I share from my own experience in this book and what I have witnessed by watching my family's journey over my lifetime, along with observing thousands of clients in my time as an accountant, over the past 14 years.

I've seen a lot of people make money, some doubling their wealth in a year (some, every year) and I've also seen the devastation of people losing significant amounts of money. As an accountant, I have a front-row seat to see what works (and what doesn't) when it comes to wealth creation. This has helped me to shape my own journey and this book that you are reading.

I want to give you some context to how I've put this book together, and the *Wealth for Life framework* I've created. The 9 steps I share are organised into 3 different sections: **Foundations, Structures and Growth.**

It starts with three foundational steps. The first is setting the vision for yourself and your family. Without a vision, goals or aspirations, there is very little help an adviser can give you – because they don't understand what end you have in mind. Vision is one of the most important

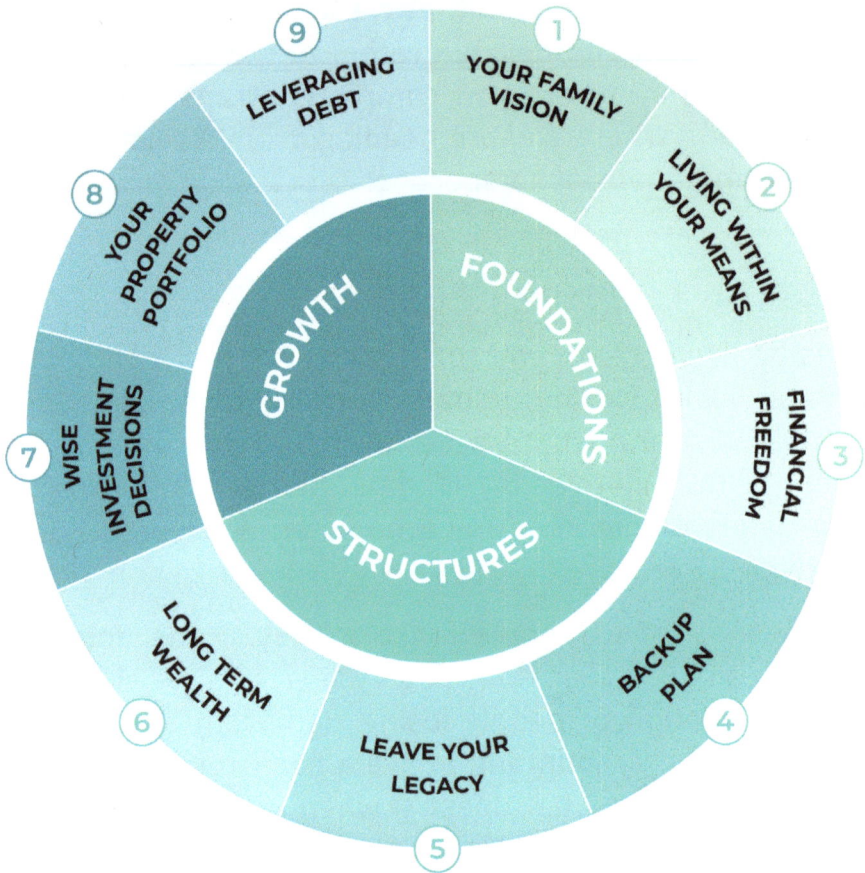

steps and takes the place as Step 1. In fact, I've put all of the steps together intentionally in the order they are numbered. The idea is you will read and implement it chronologically, referring back to sections when needed.

The second step is 'Living within your means'. In this Step, the idea is to look at the concept of spending less than you earn, in order to build wealth. I also suggest some simple and practical ways you can create a household budget to make sure you keep an eye and automated restraints on the spending part, while working out ways to grow the income you pull from your business.

The third and final foundational step is about financial freedom. This involves setting a goal for you to achieve for investment income and a net wealth target, which will give you some numbers to aim for.

After the foundational steps, we then need to put the right structures in place.

The first structure, Step 4 in the journey, is making sure you have a backup plan in place, otherwise known as insurance. Things always don't go as planned, and if something happens like the inability to work, a serious accident or illness, or even death, then we want to make sure the people we love are taken care of.

Step 5 is about leaving your legacy, and specifically, I mean estate planning. It's understood that around 60% of Australians die without a Will. As a business owner, even if you do have a simple Will, it's probably not detailed enough to deal with all your structures, such as companies and trusts. I go into detail in this section of the book about specific things that you may need as a business owner in order to have a complete estate plan.

The last structure, Step 6, focuses on your long-term wealth structure, or superannuation. Superannuation gets me excited because it is such a low-tax environment. At Inspire, we've helped many business owners navigate the space of self-managed superannuation funds as a means of boosting their wealth while also benefiting their business growth plans along the way. It's not something to ignore or defer to when you're older – and I'll go into some unique ways that you can use a self-managed super fund to your advantage.

The last three steps talk about growth.

The first of these growth steps, or Step 7, is making sure you make wise investment decisions. I discuss the different types of investments you may want to consider, and more importantly, show you the power of compound returns.

Step 8 is about property. Property makes up a very high proportion of our clients' investment portfolios and there's good reason for that. I will cover the ins and outs, especially from a tax perspective on property investment principles.

The last step, number 9, is all about leveraging debt. Debt doesn't need to be a taboo word, and it can be extremely effective in helping us to build wealth when you are leveraging other people's (i.e., the bank's) money and getting a better net return on your own money. Leveraging debt and borrowing money, while it may attract a bit more risk, can double, triple or quadruple the returns compared to not borrowing money and paying cash in full for property.

That is an overview of the 9 steps to creating wealth. After each step, there will be a short implementation checklist, and in certain places throughout the book, a worksheet for you to fill in Please use this and make sure you implement strategies that are the most relevant to you right now.

How To Get The Most Out Of This Book

Paul Dunn, a mentor of mine, once told me the story about one of his friends and clients Wally. Wally ran a pet shop specialising in training parrots to talk. Wally was mentoring another business owner and, as a strategy to get more customers, he recommended that he draw a big arrow on the road pointing at the shop.

I'm not sure whether Wally suggested that in jest or whether it was serious, but the business owner did it anyway. The result was a lot more attention to the business from drivers on the road, and both enquiries and sales increase. The lesson Paul shared out of that is that he often sees too many business owners hesitate to implement good advice or suggestions (or *any* advice or suggestions). He coined the phrase 'FTI Disease' which stands for 'failure to implement' disease.

FTI Disease is the biggest risk to your wealth creation journey. This book is meant to give you some great education from experience and suggestions, and they are intended to fuel your thoughts and inspire you to act on what you feel you need to do.

I do want to be very clear that this is not a 'one size fits all' solution, or tailored and specific financial advice. In fact, I'm personally not a licensed financial planner, and therefore not qualified to give financial product advice to anyone, although what I'm sharing here are common sense approaches to wealth creation and how I've tailored them as a business owner in my personal circumstances.

But I do want you to take action on the different steps of creating wealth for yourself and your family. Please reach out to our team at inspire (https://inspire.accountants/chat) if you need recommendations of some good people to work with on the Steps where we may not be able to help you implement it ourselves.

The Difference Between Business Wealth & Family Wealth

As business owners, we can often get so absorbed in our businesses that we neglect many other things in our lives. I think that we might all be able to relate to that neglect in some way. It may be our personal health,

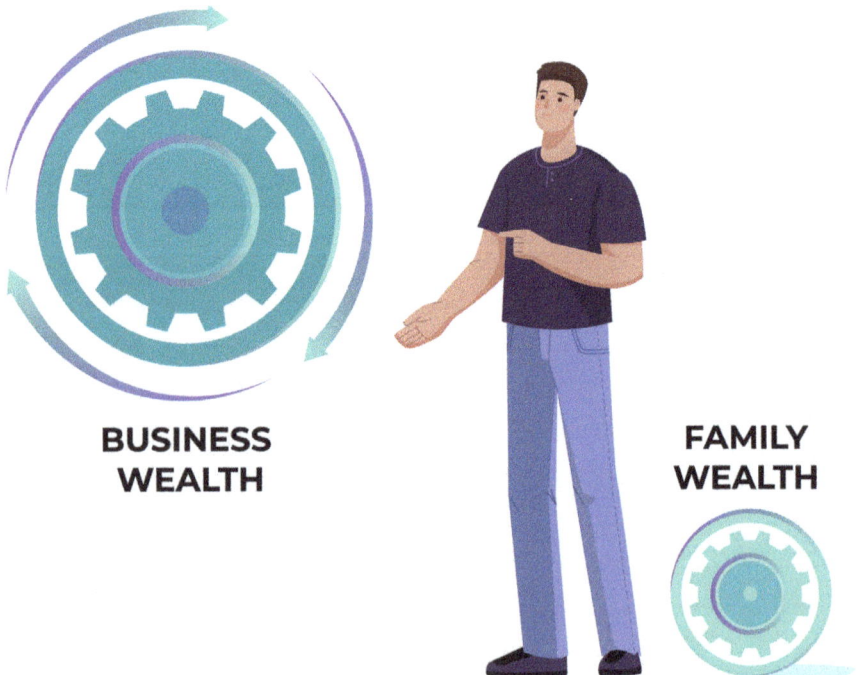

BUSINESS WEALTH

FAMILY WEALTH

our family relationships, our spouse, our leisure time – whatever it is or has been for you.

What I want to bring attention to in this book is not to focus solely on building wealth through your business, but on taking the profit that your business generates and investing that profit into other investment vehicles.

We have all had the warning of 'all our eggs being in one basket' and I've seen too many examples of someone's business being their only or the largest asset in their family alongside their family home. But, what if the business was to be thrown a curly one, as we've seen in recent years, and be brought to a standstill?

The hard work, sweat, and tears of that business owner, together with any value in their business, may be compromised. Watching a business owner with a great business to be sent back to square one from a personal wealth perspective because something wiped out their business is one of the hardest things for me to see.

Now, I did mention the family home earlier. What I also have seen too many times, is that when a business owner *does* lose their business, they often lose their house along with it. This may be because the business had debt, and the security for that debt was attached to the house. When the debt gets out of control and the business can't pay it back, the lender can look to recover the funds from the house itself.

Sometimes funding might need security like a house to be involved, or the business owner might be okay with taking a high level of risk, but I feel that it is important for us to make sure that our wellbeing and the wellbeing of our family isn't compromised when something bad happens.

But what if you were to get this right? For the first few months – or maybe years – of running a business, most people might take the bare minimum in terms of paying themselves a salary or taking drawings from their business. The rest goes back in as an investment into the business. There should (hopefully) come a point where the business doesn't need so much cash invested back into it, which means that the money coming out of the business can provide for your family's living needs and more.

I feel that the ultimate goal of running a business is to provide more freedom of time or freedom of money for the business owner and their family. So, as the business grows further than this, the profit from the business should exceed what that family needs to live on.

Now, you've got a choice here:

1) **Everything above your living costs could be invested; or**

2) **You could use some of that excess profit to increase or enhance your lifestyle, such as holidays, toys, fun experiences, cars, and gifts, while at the same time, investing a decent share of the excess profit for your family's future.**

My school of thought is Option 2. One of the reasons that I have that opinion is because I believe that life needs to be enjoyed as a journey. It is not some destination of

retirement or endpoint where you have to squirrel away enough money to live on while doing nothing to enjoy the 'now'.

Another of my reasons for this is that I don't believe I will ever retire in the sense where one day I will suddenly lose interest in, or stop, working at all. Even if it's part-time, I don't see myself stopping. Why? Because I thoroughly enjoy what I do, the relationships I have, and the opportunities that I see in business – whether that is through Inspire or otherwise.

If that's the case, I will likely be making enough of a living through my 'work' so that I don't *need* to rely on investment income to live. This means that income can be earmarked for my family's legacy, or my contribution to causes that I value, throughout my life.

Also, as a business owner, you have chosen one of what I believe is the most challenging pursuits there is. Where else do you get challenged and have to wear so many hats that there is no formal training for? Where there is often no path before us, for the way you do things, and we have to carve out our own approach?

On the other hand, business is one of the primary ways that millionaires and billionaires are made. So, while you have a great challenge on your hands in making your business successful, when it is done right, it can be extremely rewarding financially. In fact, I don't think there is any other way of earning money that can propel your wealth creation journey faster than running a highly profitable business.

I hope I have explained clearly why I feel that, as a business owner, you have a duty not only to build your business but keep an eye on building your personal wealth as well.

Just a sidenote: the purpose of this book is not to talk about growing the profit in your business. Please read my other book *Total Financial Control* if you would like my perspectives and experience on growing both my own and many other client's businesses.

The Mindset of Creating Wealth

I'm not going to dive too deeply into mindset of wealth creation, but there are a few things that I do want to share from my own journey as an encouragement to other people who may have been in a similar situation to me.

Mental glass ceilings

The first thing I want to mention is that I have had multiple mental glass ceilings of income or wealth throughout my journey. In the first few months of creating Inspire, I started training and coaching with an accounting industry coach in Brisbane, Rob Nixon.

I had literally started my accounting firm just a few months earlier. I had a handful of clients that I purchased from my previous employer, and I was in the room with other accounting firm owners who had been in business for 10, 15, or 20 years.

The coaching experience was very transparent. Every single firm in my group shared intimate details of the financial performance of their firm, along with other non-financial key KPI's of an accounting firm. Now, a couple of things stood out about that experience for me.

At the time of starting my firm, the numbers that were shared by the other established firms in that coaching session were mind-blowing to me. The firms earned millions of dollars of revenue each year and hundreds of thousands of dollars in profit. It was extremely eye-opening, whereas my revenue at the time was lucky to reach $20,000 or $30,000 in a month.

The other thing Rob used to mention in his presentations was that his vision for an accounting firm owner was that they earn more than $1,000,000 each year, while working less than 500 client hours, known more commonly as 'billable' hours.

To me at the time, these numbers were so far away from where I was, that they seemed unachievable. But, somehow, I reached a point where I have pushed through each of those ceilings or barriers that I perceived along the way.

Looking back now, part of me doesn't know how I made it to where I've got to, but I do feel like the best answer to 'how' I achieved it is that I put one foot in front of the other, I listened to good advice along the way, I implemented what I felt was right at the time (often making mistakes), and weathered every storm that was thrown at me, knowing that eventually, I'd get through it. At the same time, I am sure right now that I have a perception of yet another glass ceiling which I will again push through.

So, if you've got the same thought process around not being able to achieve a revenue or profit goal in your business, or reaching a net wealth position for yourself personally, then I encourage you to remember that the limit is only in your head, and that with the right thinking, support, and strategy, you can push through it.

Self-Worth & Net Worth

One of the other limiting beliefs I've had to deal with is the concept of self-worth for net worth. What I mean by this is that as our family wealth grew over the years, I experienced imposter syndrome or lack of faith in my ability to grow and maintain the current level of wealth. I personally needed to spend time with more people where my higher business profit level and my higher net wealth level were 'normal' instead of 'mind-blowing'.

I recall a well-told saying from Jim Rohn that "you are the average of the five closest people to you". I needed to work on my character as a business owner, father, husband, and investor with this higher level of income, net wealth and, in a way, responsibility. I ended up finding a great group of people in Entrepreneurs Organisation Queensland, which is part of a global organisation with Steps across the world who have helped me grow immensely as a person.

So, if you are struggling with anything like the imposter syndrome or self-worth relating to what profit or net wealth you can achieve, then please make sure to spend time around people where your targets are normal net worths for them. This will help you to expand into what you are capable of achieving.

Now, just one last thing that comes to mind before we get into the meaty stuff: I want to encourage you to imagine huge possibilities when it comes to your wealth. This is not for greed or to obsess over it, but rather to say that with the right ingredients anything is possible.

Soon, in Part 1, we are going to be talking about vision. This refers to having a vision for you, your life, and your family's life. If you really do want something, then please remember that it *will* be possible in some way. Don't limit your potential by what you think might be achievable right now.

Download Wealth for Life Book Resources

Throughout the book I mention many tools, templates and checklists that we use to talk with clients around these topics.

I've put together these resources that bring this book to life at the following link:

https://inspire.accountants/wealth-for-life-resources

Or you can use the QR Code below to go to the website:

PART 1:
Foundations

W e will kick off the book, and Part 1, with a bit of goal setting. Don't skip this bit and the associated exercises, as the rest of the book will be a lot harder to connect with if you don't have your family vision and your goals in place first.

Step 2 covers some basics around creating wealth, and a closer look at how you set up a simple, automated household budget.

We will then finish Part 1 with Step 3, which involves working out how much you need to have in investments to have the choice of whether you want to work again. This will give you a tangible number and a clear goal to work towards on your investment journey.

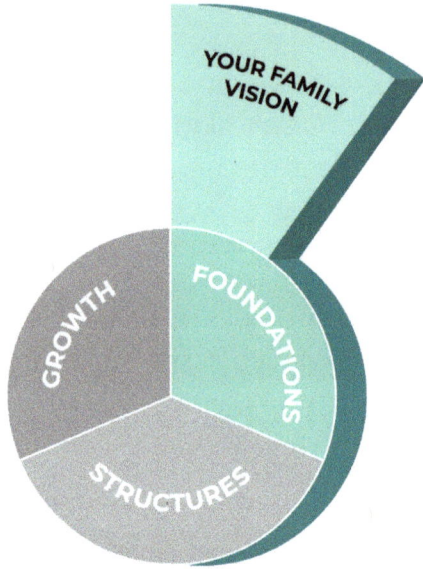

Step 1:
Your Family Vision

"Your vision will become clear only when you can look into your own heart. Who looks outside, dreams, who looks inside, awakes."

Carl Jung

Having a vision for your life means having direction for what you want to be doing, where you want to be, what you want to achieve, what value you want to add to other people in your life, and what legacy you want to leave.

Creating a vision for me doesn't come naturally, although the importance of it to lead an impactful life is communicated in many personal development books and courses. That impact can be on you as your own person, your family, your friends, your clients, your team, your community, the world. Whatever it is, the best bit about it is that you get to decide the what, who, when, where and why.

Vision is extremely important when we also talk about concepts around wealth creation, living your ideal lifestyle, and what you want your life to look like. As an adviser to thousands of clients over the years, the easiest people to help and in fact work with, are not the wealthiest clients, or the people who seem to have it all together, but the people who are super clear on their intentions and goals in life.

It is much easier and more engaging to help people get to a specific outcome than to just generally assist someone with their tax, while advising around improving their business, or their journey of creating wealth. Therefore, the first step in creating wealth for life is to spend an appropriate amount of time thinking about and crafting the vision *for* your life. It is intentionally the first step because, without this in place, the other eight steps become difficult – or even pointless – to move through.

I mentioned before that this doesn't come naturally to me, and maybe it isn't the highest priority or the first thing on your list to do in the free time you have. In this step, I will share some tools I use, some experiences I've had, and what I've seen work with many other friends and clients to date to make it an easy and hopefully enjoyable process.

If you are tempted to skip past this first step, please reconsider doing that, as I guarantee it will make the rest of the book more comprehensive and have a better impact on helping you achieve your goals.

Create Your Bucket List

The first exercise I suggest you do is to map out your Bucket List.

This is the first thing my wife Stevie and I did on our initial relationship retreat. I'll walk you through the process that we completed. It was 2015 and I had recently returned from a business event.

One of the steps that we workshopped together in the event was to create our Bucket Lists. The format was simple: there were rows and columns. In the columns were different areas of life, such as:

- Business or career,
- Personal development and learning,
- Wealth,
- Lifestyle,
- Travel

And for the rows it showed different measures of time:

- 90 days
- 1 year
- 3 to 5 years
- 5 to 10 years
- 10 to 25 years

	PERSONAL / LIFESTYLE	FAMILY / RELATIONSHIPS	COMMUNITY / CONTRIBUTION	BUSINESS / WEALTH
10 - 25 Year ASPIRATIONS				
3 - 5 Year ACHIEVEMENTS				
12 Month GOALS				
90 Day Actions	NEW RITUALS	NEW RITUALS	NEW RITUALS	NEW RITUALS
	NEW ASSETS	NEW ASSETS	NEW ASSETS	NEW ASSETS
	STOP	STOP	STOP	STOP

inspire™ BUCKET LIST

The Bucket List template is available for download on the Wealth For Life book resources page (page 19).

The goal was to brainstorm things that came to your mind on the goals, dreams, and aspirations you had for yourself within each of those categories, for each of those timelines.

For me, the next 90 days, the next year, and even the next three to five years were quite simple. It was the longer-term goals, which I hadn't really thought about before that, that were great to give some forward thought to.

I was also familiar with planning out business or wealth goals, but I hadn't had much thought comparatively in the lifestyle, travel, personal development, or family sections. It was great for me to think about what was possible for the future and what I'd really like out of life.

So, I took this tool home and, within a few weeks, Stevie and I were on that relationship retreat and the Bucket List tool came out.

We each spent a good couple of hours filling this out for ourselves independently. While of course we had shared goals and visions for our family, I felt it was important to do it separately first. That way, we weren't influenced by each other's goals, limitations, or biases. It was a great chance to think, "What do I selfishly want out of life?"

After we had each spent time doing our own lists, we got ready for dinner and headed to the restaurant at Spicers. It turned out to be one of the best date nights we'd ever had, because we spent time sharing one by one each section on our list. One of us started first, sharing what we'd like personally out of life. Then the other would share on the personal side.

The next sharing was in the business or career section where one of us would reveal their particular dreams and aspirations, and the next person would share after that. While some of the goals and dreams we had spoken about in some detail before, there were quite a few that were news to each of us. This was thanks to the independent work we had done beforehand. It was cool to discover some of Stevie's goals, that I was now inspired to help her achieve.

I do encourage you to do this with your spouse. Even if you've got children with whom this would be appropriate, involving them in the process to do their own Bucket List would be great, too. Don't forget that 'sharing' step after it's finished. Not only does that reinforce the goals you've set for yourself, but also you get your spouse and family on board, too.

Some of these goals, especially lifestyle, wealth creation, and business or career goals, will be very important when you are discussing your plans with advisers. So please keep a copy of the bucket list handy. This is not only to review your progress, but to also be able to share these with your advisers as and when it makes sense to share.

Exercise: Create Your Bucket List

In terms of doing this exercise, the link here will take you to the Bucket List template that you can copy to a new google sheet and customise however you like:

https://inspire.accountants/wealth-for-life-resources

Because it was so effective, I recommend doing the strategy I suggest above where you:

1. Set aside a couple of hours where you will be uninterrupted (and your spouse can do it at the same time)

2. Independently work on your bucket lists, drawing inspiration from what you believe is possible or even outrageously aspirational in your life in these different areas

3. In a semi or fully romantic setting, like a date night or after the kids go to bed, grab the Bucket Lists and one by one, a section at a time, share your dreams goals and aspirations with each other

If you don't have a spouse, then you could do this with a close friend. But regardless, it is a super important step before reading the rest of the book especially if you haven't already got a well-thought-out and documented set of goals for your life.

I'd also love to hear your feedback on how this went for you, and whether you've got any cool tips or things that worked well that you feel I could include when I share this exercise in the future. Feel free to send me an email at ben@inspire.accountants with the subject line 'Bucket List' with your feedback on the exercise.

Clear Communication (Regular Meetings)

The next thing that has helped in achieving a great outcome for Stevie and my relationship is to build communication rhythms into our life. We often have detailed communication rhythms in our business, so why not do it in our personal life?

I got this brainwave by having a look at what we do in my business Inspire when it comes to team meetings and communication. Through years of researching the best practice for leading, growing, and running high-performance teams, we had a series of meetings that we did every day, week, month, quarter, and year.

We've taken these concepts from things such as Gino Wickman's book *Traction*, and Jim Collin's book *Scaling Up*. Each meeting has a specific agenda, start time, finish time, and desired outcome, which are set in advance. At Inspire, we use software called Traction Tools to manage these agendas, issues, the to-do list from each meeting, and to progress on those 'to-do's'.

Over the page, you will see how we applied our rhythms on a daily, weekly, monthly, and quarterly basis (left hand side). On the right-hand side, you can see how Stevie and I apply similar communication rhythms to our personal life and relationship.

BUSINESS RHYTHMS

Daily

We hold a morning huddle, at 7:47am to discuss:
- Check in on our key KPI's
- What's on that day
- If I need any help

Weekly

We hold various meetings such as:
- Workflow meeting – to discuss the status of major projects
- Sales meeting – to discuss key sales activities, and update the pipeline
- Marketing meeting – discussing key marketing activities, review future events, review and discuss marketing collateral
- Thank You Circle – the full team catches up on a Friday and we share what we're grateful for that week from our colleagues
- Leadership Meeting - this is a weekly meeting for leaders in the business to catch up and chat through any issues or opportunities

Monthly

Our monthly rhythms include:
- Budget Review - discuss the budget versus actual for the previous month, and make any adjustments to the quarterly budget as a result
- Business Planning – a half day each month, where the partners and managers catch up to discuss high level strategic planning

Quarterly

I say quarterly, although add inspire we work off 3x four-month trimesters in a year instead of four quarters.
- Leadership Retreat - This is where we take the leadership team offsite to work through how we've gone in the last trimester, and what big rocks we want to set for the coming trimester
- Team Retreat - the team retreat is for sharing the vision for new people and reminding existing team members of the vision that we're working towards from here through to 10 years away. we work our way down to 3 years goals 1 year goals and the next 120 day goals as a business and individually

FAMILY RHYTHMS

Daily

We have a morning coffee together before I go to work - just checking on what each other are up to for the day and any help we each need.

Weekly

Each week we try to go on a date night, with my parents taking care of the kids once I've gone to bed.
It's a chance to spend some time on their own without the kids.
It is a good time to review how you are going with your short term goals, especially ones that show progress week to week such as number of times you've been to the gym, or quality time spent with the kids.
Also taking the leaf out of what we do at work each Friday for the thank you circle, we aim to give a bit of gratitude to each other for stuff that each of us has done that week if that we're thankful for.

Monthly

In terms of a monthly personal rhythm, we don't do anything too different to what we would ordinarily do in a weekly date night.
The difference is our context is looking at the next month coming up for travel or events or financial stuff that we need to prepare for. Real examples of this has been making sure we've got enough cash ready to go for settlement of a property purchase, or getting ready for a baby that's coming along with furniture or a pram etc. ideally anything that's had a bit of notice is spoken about and budgeted for months in advance rather than the month of the expense.

Quarterly

In terms of quarterly rhythms, ideally this is done as a weekend or overnight away.
Since we've had kids we haven't managed to do this without the kids unfortunately, but I'm hoping as they get older we get back to those now it's child free weekends away with the help of the grandparents.
Regardless this is a good chance to go back into that vision planning mode - where you take your bucket list with you, and hopefully celebrate as you tick some things off.
And the most important thing about a quarterly retreat is that you book the next one before you finish the current quarterly retreat. (The same thing should go with holidays where you book your next holiday before your current one finishes.)

Exercise: Communication Rhythms

While this is fresh on your mind, go and block out your first relationship retreat in your calendar. You get bonus points for instantly booking the accommodation.

Ideally, this is two nights away, so you can spend a good amount of time together connecting with your spouse. Even if you don't get to the Bucket List soon or beforehand, make sure this is the first exercise that you do on that retreat.

If these communication rhythms make sense - and you can adapt them for yourself - pop them in the calendar, and even have some fun with the date nights where you take turns in organising them. Weekly date nights might sound excessive, but with young kids, they are something Stevie and I look forward to. It gives us a chance to just chill out without that constant awareness and energy that kids require. (A big thanks to my mum and dad who look after the kids while we're out!) And lastly, don't forget to 'BARFAR': book a retreat from a retreat.

Conclusion

Once you've got your Bucket List finalised and your communication rhythms set in the calendar, it's time to plan out the rest of the 8 steps to creating wealth for life. You can always refer back to your Bucket List to change and adjust your plans to suit as you read this book, but always refer back to it as your plan to remind you of where you're heading.

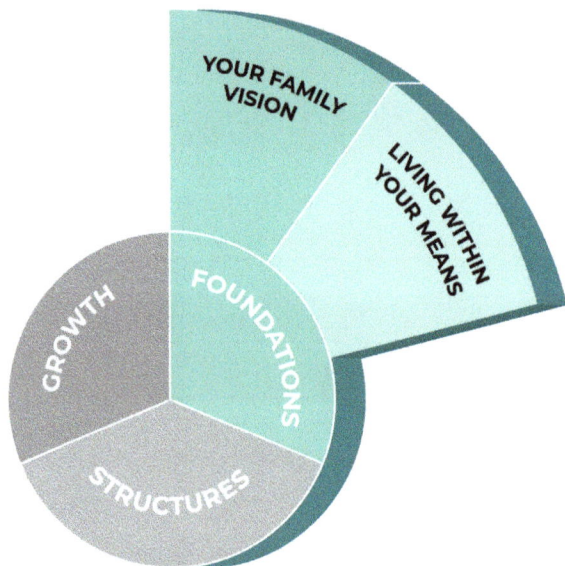

Step 2:
Living Within Your Means

"Annual income twenty pounds, annual expenditure nineteen pounds, nineteen and six, result happiness. Annual income twenty pounds, annual expenditure twenty pounds, nought and six, result misery."

Charles Dickens

When I was a lot younger, I remember seeing other family friends or family members who had done a great job of creating wealth in their lifetime. I didn't know anyone who was 'rich list' wealthy that comes to mind, but there were two people I remember who stood out at getting something right when it came to their wealth.

One of them was my grandfather, who started a removalist company and grew it into a decent small business over decades of owning and running it. When my grandmother was diagnosed with cancer, he immediately stepped back and retired earlier than he had expected while his sons managed the business. He was able to still earn an income from what he had set up, but was able to also care for my grandmother while she was recovering and through to remission.

From that point onwards, he had effectively retired and spent his time creating a beautiful space on the acreage property they had in Warner, north of Brisbane.

Another example I noticed was a friend at school, whose dad had started and built multiple businesses. As an example, one of those businesses was into importing and selling rainwater tanks when there was a huge drought and water restrictions in Queensland. I now know that the definition of this is 'an entrepreneur', but at the time what I saw was his ability to work flexible hours and spend time with the kids after school or on the weekends. I also remember that he drove a pretty cool Commodore and was able to trade up when the new one came out every couple of years.

Why I'm mentioning both of these stories is that they inspired me to know that wealth creation was in a way a tangible goal. But, at the same time, while I was still at school and working at the local Red Rooster, it felt like it was a crazy long journey to be able to come anywhere close to where these two people were.

As I went into university and full-time work, I looked into common strategies to create additional wealth. I remember at one stage I was doing full-time university, full-time work, and still working night shifts and weekend work at the retail shop Target to try and earn some extra coin.

But my research showed another way I could earn an income: by investing in shares, which my parents had done over the years. I had a crack at it myself without too much success. In fact, the very little amount I did invest in took a huge hit, as I started investing in the sharemarket about a year before the GFC (Global Financial Crisis) occurred in 2008.

Even after a few years of working, I explored starting a consulting business for accounting firms to set up their IT systems. This was after helping the boss I was working for implement systems in his firm. I thought of starting this consulting because I found the IT work rather easy.

So, I was always looking for additional ways to create income streams with the overall goal of achieving the same flexibility and choice that came with wealth I had seen growing up. But in terms of actual wealth creation strategies, I feel like I overcomplicated it when I was younger: I was always looking for the quick win or the next best thing that was going to make me a millionaire overnight.

What I have discovered, that has taken me up until recent years to realise, is that wealth creation is not something that is developed quickly or easily in most cases. Rather, it is the accumulation of multiple habits over years if not decades. Making smart decisions, and taking action when it is needed is what got most wealthy people to where they are. At the end of the day, there is a very simple formula to create wealth.

You need to earn more than you spend, and do this consistently, for a sustained amount of time. All the wealth courses, books, and ideas seem to do is overcomplicate

CREATING WEALTH

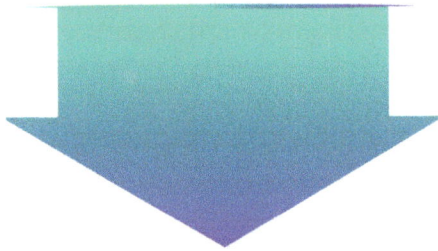

EARNING > SPENDING

that formula. So, if that is how simple it is to create wealth, then we need to know two things:

1. **How much are we earning; and**

2. **How much are we spending?**

Once we know these two things very clearly if we want to increase the speed at which we create wealth, then there are two ways to do that:

1. **Increase what we earn; or**

2. **Decrease what we spend.**

I guess the first thing to do is make sure that you're not going backwards (going backwards means reducing your savings or going into debt). If you are going backwards, you need to look into fixing that formula first. Now, we are going to explore how we increase the rate at which we create wealth, by doing each of those two things.

Increase Your Income

On the topic of increasing what you earn, I believe that business owners have the greatest control over their income. Why? Because there are a lot more levers that they can pull in their business to be able to produce more profit and cash at the end of the day.

That doesn't mean employees or retirees are unable to change this though. You could get a pay rise for working as an employee or find an additional job. You could increase the income you earn or income-producing assets, such as rent on a property, dividends on shares or managed funds, and interest on bank accounts (although at the time of writing the interest rate is extremely low that most banks are offering zero or less than 1% interest). Other ideas include starting a business, even if it's something basic like driving for Uber or cleaning after hours.

Whatever it is, if you're increasing what you're earning and not increasing what you spend at the same time, then you will be increasing the rate at which you create wealth. I also don't believe someone should be working an 80-hour week and not spending any time with their family because they've got three income streams from working. So, please keep in mind my intention here is to suggest a fair balance, while maximising your potential.

If you *are* running a business, then the goal is to work smarter not necessarily harder. You can do this by understanding the levers that really drive profitability and cash in your business. We go into detail on these topics with our product *Total Financial Control* at Inspire, where we work with business owners to help them understand the numbers that drive profit, cash and business value. If you do need a hand with this, it might be worth reaching out to see if it is something we could help you with.

Decrease Your Expenses

The next topic I want to run through with you is ideas on ways to decrease your expenses. Now, I'm a big believer in not living skint so that you hardly spend a thing. I do believe that having a quality lifestyle is important, so I'm not advocating going back to two-minute noodles for dinner, driving a crappy car, and never going out for date nights or away for holidays. If that's your thing, go for it, though.

But, to me, chasing a goal where you are compromising so much that you're not enjoying the journey, is not a goal I feel is worth chasing. This may get you to financial freedom a lot faster, but life is short – and sometimes it is made unexpectedly shorter than you think – and I feel that would be a huge regret to live the majority of my life not being able to enjoy the journey.

On the other hand, living a big lifestyle on moderate earnings would mean a very slow journey to create wealth. So, with all of these things, I feel like it is relative, and I have experienced myself going through different stages of wealth creation.

For instance, there were probably times when I was going into debt because my lifestyle was more than what I was earning. Then the next phase may have been living off 85% to 95% of my income and investing the rest. Then it may have dropped to let's say 60% of my income while investing 40%. And now with our family lifestyle, it costs us less than 40% of our income, while we pay down debt or invest 60% or more.

You may have a gut feeling for where you're currently at, but it's definitely worth working out where your current spending is compared to your income and see if there's room to move to reduce your spending.

Some ways I suggest you could explore this is:

- **Cutting off your non-vital expenses** - For instance if you have six TV streaming services, could you probably reduce this to three without having an impact on your lifestyle or leisure time

- **Bulk buying food or household needs** - There are a lot of Costco shops in Australia now which provide more value for buying bulk. Something my family has done over the past couple of years is to purchase meat by the whole animal, such as a whole lamb or pig, from our butcher which is a lot cheaper per kilo cost, even though you do need a bit more freezer space for this

- **Cook a meal versus getting UberEats** - Now again, keeping lifestyle in mind, I do enjoy the convenience and variety of getting the odd UberEats throughout the week, but if you are getting it five times a week and you could drop it to twice a week, without having a detrimental drop in lifestyle, this may save you a few grand a year

- **Restructure your debt** - This could be your own home loan or credit cards or investment debt, but regularly make sure you're on a great rate and a good loan structure to keep cash flow top of mind. I've seen clients save hundreds or thousands of dollars a month by changing from poor setups to great ones, when it comes to debt.

- **Reducing personal and business tax** - If you are working with us at Inspire, we should be doing a great job at making this happen, but things to keep in mind here is making the most of the available business structures and tax planning techniques that we use to pay the least amount of tax legally possible. This alone saves our clients an average of around $20,000 per year in tax (keeping in mind that we work solely with business owners). There are ways to reduce tax as an employee, but these are limited and they often take months or years to implement well.

We're also going to be doing an exercise next which will look at ways you might be able to discover the expenses you can reduce.

Exercise: Trim The Fat

This is an exercise I call 'trimming the fat'. This is where we look at unique ways that you may be able to reduce your regular expenses.

I want to share a story first about Stevie and my coffee drinking. We love our coffee and, unfortunately, neither of us can stand instant coffee. So, before we had a coffee machine at home, we would literally go to a cafe every single day, twice a day to get our fix. We would order a long black with a dash of cold milk, which costs around $4.50.

That means we were spending around **$18 a day** on coffee ($4.5 x 2 people x twice a day). If we work this out over a year (because we even tracked down the cafes that were open on public holidays!), we were spending $6,570 a year on coffee.

Being in business, I had put a lot of business expenses on my credit card that had awards points. I discovered one of the rewards I could purchase was a Breville coffee machines that pushed out a proper extraction of coffee. A couple of weeks later, one showed up on the kitchen bench. In terms of ongoing costs to fuel this thing with coffee beans, it costs us about $40 per kilo bag of beans each fortnight. So, that is an ongoing yearly cost of $1,040 for our coffee. The difference here between going to a cafe every day (twice a day) and making our daily coffees on the Breville is around $5,530 per year.

On its own, it's a significant amount of money. but, if we compound this amount with an 8% return on investment over 20 years (by the time we're in our early 50's), we are looking at an amount of $253,064! (And even more, in our early 70's, this strategy alone is worth a touch over $1.4 million to us). We'll touch more on the power of compound returns (or savings) in *Step 7: Wise Investment Decisions.*

Now, for your exercise:

1.   Pull up your credit card statement or bank account transactions live on your computer or phone (your personal credit card statement or bank account, showing your living expenses).

2. Scroll through the last couple of months, and look for regular / recurring expenses that you could:

    a. Reduce; or

    b. Cancel altogether

Then tally them up using the table below.

You are looking for the **total annual savings** as a result of doing this exercise.

Example exercise:

Expense saved or reduced	Saving per wk or mth	Annual Saving
Coffee (Breville instead of café)		$5,530 / year
Keep Netflix, but cancel Stan & Amazon Prime	$40 / m	$480 / year
Uber Eats twice per week instead of 5 times	$150 / wk	$7,800 / year
Total Savings		$13,810 / year

Expense saved or reduced	Saving per wk or mth	Annual Saving

Total Savings		

I love hearing the numbers of total savings when we host a workshop and do this exercise live. So, if you are inspired by your result, please shoot me an email at ben@inspire.accountants or post the following on Instagram (or the other socials) tagging me: *"I just saved $XX,XXX a year doing the #trimthefat exercise thanks @benwalkerca"*

Using An Automated Household Budget

What I want to share next is something that changed the way that Stevie and I communicated about finances. It solved a lot of the problems we were having proactively, rather than waiting for problems to appear and then having to go through the pain of experiencing and then fixing them.

This is something that we implemented years and years ago and still use to this day, even though our financial position has changed quite substantially since we first implemented this. It was born out of sheer frustration of wanting to find a very easy way that we could budget, along with the ability to communicate about money well with my spouse. This was especially important for me as a business owner who was very used to large variances in bank balances in the business.

Now I have to say that, as an accountant, I don't like the association of the word 'budget', nor do I love the process of doing one (I find it super boring). But what I do love and appreciate is the outcome and the benefits you experience from having done this well.

If you feel like this section is about to get a bit number focused (and boring), please bear with it. This alone had a significant effect on our wealth creation trajectory, but I feel, more importantly, the way that Stevie and I communicated about money.

Option 1:
ONE ACCOUNT

Option 2:
MULTIPLE ACCOUNTS

Everything goes into and out of the single account

Business Bucket

"Living Expenses" Account

Weekly Drawings

Weekly bills paid automatically

Automatic transfers

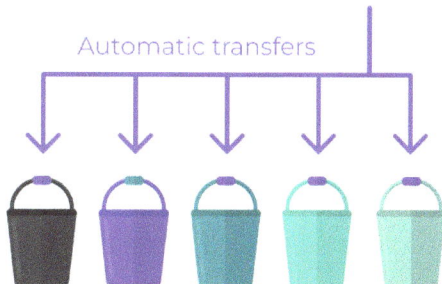

The image above shows that there are two options for running your personal banking or personal accounts. *(NOTE: We're not discussing business accounts here, just personal.)*

The first option is extreme, where you only have one account for all your income and expenses. Now, I doubt that many people at all would have one account to manage everything (usually people I speak to have at least 2 or 3 accounts), but this is to illustrate the point that it is very difficult to work out how much you have remaining in your accounts for each different type of expense that life throws at you when you use a single account only.

I want to compare this to option two. This is where you run your household expenses from multiple bank accounts. Also distinguished here is that there are automatic transfers to each of these sub-accounts or 'buckets' each week, where there is a clear purpose for each of these buckets.

Now I'm not sure how you currently organise your personal finances, but at the time, Stevie and I were having lots of confusion and misunderstandings about money. This was because each of us just assumed how much we could spend on certain things – and if there was money in the account, then there was no real communication about what that was for.

So, what it looked like was this: I transferred a fair bit of money from the business account to our personal account. This was for rent or some big purchase. But Stevie didn't know what it was for, and so she spent it on groceries or normal living expenses. Before I could do anything about it, the cash was gone.

Now that was frustrating on a couple of levels! Firstly, that now I needed to find more money for what the original intention was for (and sometimes that was difficult because this was in the first few years of Inspire where cash was tight).

Another frustration was that some weeks were great in business cash flow, so I transferred a bit more money than normal out of the business account to our personal account, which meant we were able to enjoy a nice date night or maybe go on a weekend away. But literally, a few days or a week later, things were tight again, and it was difficult for Stevie to understand why suddenly we couldn't do those things so freely.

I'm glad that things have changed quite a bit, and part of the reason for this is that we've set up this automated household budget. We've also set up similar systems in the business which help provide more stable and predictable cash flow and allow me to more easily take that business cash to provide for personal living expenses.

So, what is the automated household budget?

There are a couple of ways this needs to work. The first one is that ideally, you have a weekly amount coming out of your business as your owner's salary or drawings. This can be paid into a living expense account. Then the idea is you have pre-determined amounts that are automatically transferred to other subaccounts with specific names and uses.

Option 2:
MULTIPLE ACCOUNTS

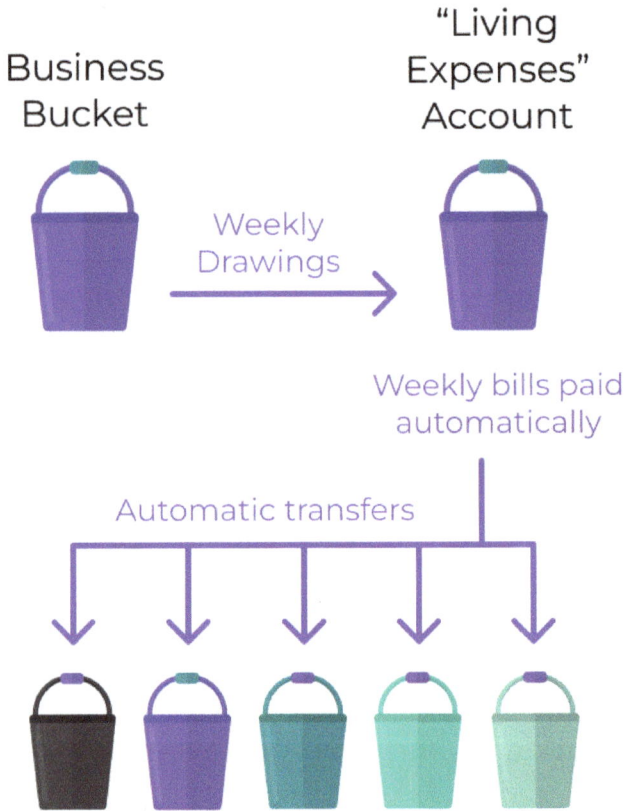

Business
Bucket

"Living
Expenses"
Account

Weekly
Drawings

Weekly bills paid
automatically

Automatic transfers

Now, here is an overview of each of the accounts that I've chosen:

SLUSH FUND

Set one up for you, and your spouse will have a separate account too. This is for you to spend as you wish* with no judgement from the other person. It's your "play" money.

ENTERTAINMENT

This is different to your slush fund - slush is intended for YOU - entertainment is for your family. Meals out, movies, outgoings etc.

TRAVEL

Have a savings account for travel and holidays over the year. Pay deposits, airfares, accomodation etc from here as it builds up.

IRREGULAR BILLS

Keep money aside for bills that pop up less frequently than each week (monthly, quarterly or annual bills). Car rego, insurance, rates, etc.

WEALTH CREATION

Send money to an account for paying down debt, or regular investing according to your strategy.

1. **Living expenses** - This is for daily or weekly expenses such as groceries, fuel, parking, pet costs etc. Make sure you only include personal expenses here instead of anything paid for by the business. Your rent or weekly mortgage repayment equivalent can come out of this account, too.

2. **Slush Fund** – The idea here is that there is a slush fund each for you and your spouse, and each week the same amount of money gets paid into this account for you to spend as you wish, with no judgement from the other person. This is your play money, whether it's paying for a boy's weekend, something here you need to save up for that's for you only to enjoy, your haircuts or gym membership. It's where the 'you' stuff gets paid from.

3. **Entertainment** - The entertainment account is similar to a slush fund in that it is for entertainment but the context here is that it's for you **and** your spouse **and** your family as well. So, think of date nights, meals out, going to the movies, taking the family to the zoo. This is the account that gets enjoyed with your family as a whole.

4. **Travel** - The name is written on the tin of this account, where the purpose of it is to travel as a family. You will pay your airfares or accommodation from this account. A good nudge, if it's been too long since a holiday, is that there should be quite a few hundred or a few thousand dollars in this account. Ideally, by the time you are heading away that there is already another few hundred or more

back in the account for things to do while you are away and meals that you might have out, as these can very quickly add up, especially if the travel is to a fancy location. You don't want to end up at a nice location and not be able to do the scuba dive or the boat trip or the zoo because you haven't set aside some cash for it. So, having enough spending money *while you are on your holiday* is also a purpose of this account (not just the airfares).

5. **Irregular Bills** - I couldn't think of a sexier name for this one, but this account is for any bill that is less frequent than weekly. This includes anything that is fortnightly, monthly, quarterly, or annually. Car registration, insurance, council rates, body corporate, health insurance or similar gets paid from this account. This is the account that receives the most money every week, and it often has a large amount in it – but that's a great thing because I want to avoid having three or four large bills coming at once and then stressing to find a few thousand dollars that it might take to clear them, rather than having it set aside already to pay.

6. **Wealth Creation** - The last account that I use is a wealth creation account, which is currently our mortgage offset account. Any leftover money we don't need for the above purposes gets shifted to the offset account each week, which offsets debt and reduces interest expense on our home loan. From time to time, we will use this money to make investments such as to put a deposit on the property, make a superannuation contribution, or

invest in a business or shares. But even sitting in the offset account it is making a difference to reduce your interest expense that is non-tax deductible against your home loan.

Any other account that you see fit - My list above is not an exhaustive list, and in fact, we have used other savings accounts in the past to set aside a weekly amount. For instance, when we were having our first child Rose, we set aside between $100 - $200 a week so that we could purchase prams, cots, and other baby equipment closer to when Rose was born. You can customise any other account you want and make it your own, but if big expenses are coming up, saving up beforehand this way can be a fantastic way to do it in small bites.

Exercise: Create Your Automated Budget

Now, your goal is to create your automated household budget and to set up the accounts that are required for you and your family.

I have prepared an Excel spreadsheet that I used to create our own. You can use it as a template to build out your budget. You'll find the link here:

https://inspire.accountants/wealth-for-life-resources

There are a few tabs on this excel spreadsheet.

The first is the **income versus expenses tab**, where you can see on a high level if you're earning more than you're spending and how much that is.

The next tab is the **budget summary tab**, where you record what type of accounts you are using. You can even record the BSB and account number, so that you can track this easily in your Internet banking. (Also note that you can usually rename or nickname your bank accounts in your internet banking, depending on the bank. This will provide you with ongoing clarity about which account is for which purpose.)

The last tab is the **budget details tab**. Here, I've given some hints on the type of expenses that you might have under each account. You can put in how much and how often you pay each expense. The spreadsheet will calculate how much the weekly equivalent is for that whole account.

Once you've filled out the budget detail tab, it should populate the budget summary tab, and that should be what is used to set your automated weekly transfers.

Purpose / Name	BSB	Account No	Weekly Allocation	Type	Card
					(Visa Debit)
Living Expenses	64000	10011001	$437	Transaction	Yes
Entertainment	64000	10011002	$115	Transaction	Yes
Slush Fund - You	64000	10011003	$150	Transaction	Yes
Slush Fund - Spouse	64000	10011004	$150	Transaction	Yes
Irregular Bills	64000	10011005	$353	Sav	
Travel	64000	10011006	$200	Sav	
Other	64000	10011007	$0	Sav	
		Total	$1,405		

As an example, you might have $3,000 per week going from your business account, into your living expenses account. The next day your automated transfers happen (using the above screenshot as an example), which sends:

- **$115 to the entertainment account**

- **$150 to your slush fund**

- **$150 to your spouse's slush fund**

- **$353 to irregular bills account**

- **$200 to travel account**

- **Your mortgage or rent of $800 a week is taken out**

- **$909 is transferred to your offset account for wealth creation**

- **Leaving $323 which is what you need in your living expenses account**

This would mean it costs your family $1,291 in living expenses plus your mortgage or rent of $800 per week to live. You're saving $909 a week in your offset account or the equivalent of $47,268 a year, and you are increasing your net wealth by this saving.

Once you've worked out the amounts per week (like the above example), the next step is to set up the automated transfers from your business into your living expenses account, and then from your living expense account into those sub-accounts. Just a tip: you may want to start with $1,000 or so cash in your regular bills account. Why? Because it may catch you off guard if a big bill comes in soon after you start this system. Once you've implemented this system, the benefit now is that you and your spouse know what purpose every dollar in your bank is for.

NOTE: I do not mention tax here in the amounts to transfer for each account. Inspire's strategy is to account and pay for tax (business and personal) from the business' cash flow.

Now, this exercise of working out what living expenses it takes to run your household is important for the next step, as the whole purpose is to work out what it will take for you to reach financial freedom based on your cost of living. So, please see it as a prerequisite to *Step 3*, or at least it will make *Step 3* much more tangible than using estimates.

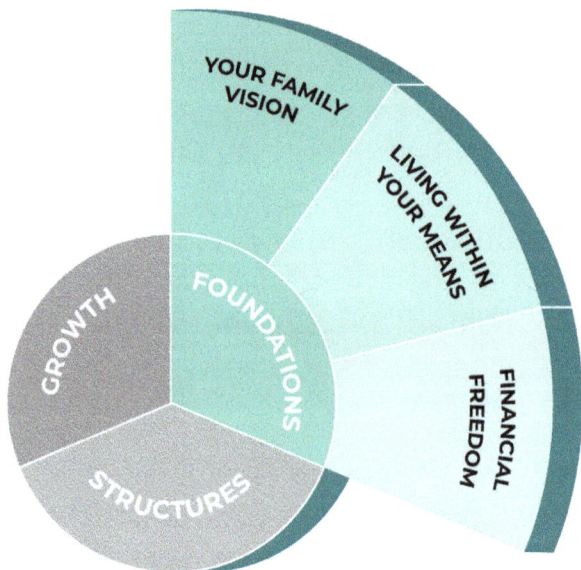

YOUR FAMILY VISION

LIVING WITHIN YOUR MEANS

FINANCIAL FREEDOM

GROWTH

FOUNDATIONS

STRUCTURES

Step 3:
Financial Freedom

"True wealth is having the freedom of choice to live life on your own terms and to be able to put your family first."

Ben Walker

I have never related to the idea of retirement in the sense that I will completely give up work. This is because I have a strong belief that you should truly enjoy what you do for a living, at least most of the time. Therefore, to me, the goal is to build freedom into my lifestyle: the freedom to do what I want, with whom I want, when I want. I see my role at Inspire, and the support that we give our clients, as part of me living that goal.

I also want to build some serious fun around the work I do – travel, lifestyle, down-time, rest, and fun. To do that, I am personally working towards achieving financial freedom. This means that our lifestyle is paid for completely from passive investments. In my opinion, this is true financial freedom.

A simpler way to say this is that your investments are paying for your living expenses so that you don't *have* to work to provide for them. The purpose of this step is to give you the tools and methods to work out what it will take to reach this goal of financial freedom for yourself and your family.

Calculating Financial Freedom

This is important because, in our wealth creation journey, I feel like we need goals or milestones to work towards, so that we are able to check if we are 'on track' or not. We need to work out how much we need in invested assets to provide fair living expenses. The formula for working that out is as follows:

Annual Living Costs   **Rate of Return (as a %)**

$$\$ \div$$

YOUR "MAGIC NUMBER" TO REACH FINANCIAL FREEDOM

$$= \$$$

In the previous step, we worked out what our annual living costs are – and I'm hoping you did the exercise of creating your household budget. So, by now, you should know how much money it takes to run your household, or at least have a good idea of it.

Let's do an example here of a financial freedom calculation. If we take the magic number I had in my example in *Step 2* of a household costing $1,291 per week, excluding a mortgage or rent, then this works out to be $67,132 per year. Now, we need to divide this annual living costs number by our estimated rate of return on our investments.

Divide the above number by:

- **2% or 0.02 if you want to be super conservative**

- **4% or 0.04 if you want to be conservative**

- **8% or 0.08 if you want to take some risk, for a decent return**

- **11.8% or 0.118 if you want to replicate the average return of ASX All Ords since 1900**

(You can customise this for any rate of return – even, for instance, if your investments are returning 20% each year, then that would be divided by 0.2)

In the example I use here, I'm going to use an 8% estimated return. This means I need to divide $67,132 (my living expenses) by 0.08 (which is 8% as a decimal). (I'm hoping that I will end up with a much higher return annually than 8% on my investments, though, over the long term.) The result of this produces a number of **$839,150.**

Now, we need to adjust this for tax. To make this simple for all the scenarios here, let's use an average tax rate of 25%. This means we need to take the number above and divide it by 0.75 (which is 1 minus 0.25 or 25%). This gives the answer of **$1,118,866.**

This means that I will need **$1,118,866** in invested assets, earning 8% per year less a 25% average tax rate to provide for my living expenses.

Mind you, just like investment preferences and target returns are very specific to a person, so is tax. For instance, I am still a few decades away from my superannuation being in 'pension' mode and being taxed on 0% on its earnings, but we've got plenty of clients in their 60's, who are living off their super funds, and their investment income is being taxed at 0%. If that was the case, then there is no adjustment you will need to make to your magic number here for tax. The 25% tax rate I used is a guess at what most people would ordinarily pay if they are earning between $80k – $150k as a family.

I also mentioned that this excludes mortgage or rent, and you may still have that outgoing or expense now or even years into the future. So, if I want to forecast this magic number while paying off my mortgage and that mortgage is $1,000,000, then I will need to clear that mortgage *and* have $1,118,866 in invested assets.

You can customise this calculation however you'd like, but before you do that, I'd like to throw another idea out there: I want to talk about a **traffic light system** when we're referring to financial freedom numbers.

Traffic Lights For Wealth

Base Line

Luxury

Baller

When I share the exercise above, I often get asked a lot of different questions where people are going deep into the detail and trying to pick it apart.

The goal here is that it's not an exact science, but it's better than having no target to aim for at all – and it is always dependent on what your current living expenses are at the moment. So, what I would suggest is that you have multiple targets for your financial freedom numbers. Again, you can customise this to what you'd like, but here are mine:

Red = Base Line

This Red 'Base Line' is the target to have invested assets that provide for your current level of lifestyle. That may not be your ideal lifestyle in the future, but it would be great to enjoy this without *having* to work. In this scenario, my target does not include the mortgage I have on my home, as I just want to work towards this initial goal of covering my living expenses.

In my example, this was $67,132 divided by 0.08 (investment return) and divide that by 0.75 (tax adjustment) = **$1,118,866**.

Orange = Luxury Level

The next level is the colour orange, and this is a luxury level in my opinion. the investing target here includes a decent amount of lifestyle dollars to do things like travel, enjoy nice restaurants, take part in some cool experiences with you and your family.

It might be $50K to 100K higher per year in expenses than the red baseline. It is a greater level of luxury compared to say your red target, but there's still room to move up to baller level. Plus, at this level, I would want my investments to be paying my mortgage off, too. For the purpose of this exercise, let's assume that my mortgage repayments are $6,000 per month.

Using my example, let's work this out being [$67,132 + $50,000 (lifestyle) + $72,000 (mortgage)] divided by 0.08 and divide that by 0.75 = **$3,152,200**.

This is starting to get to a significant number now. Plus, I would not need to consider paying off the mortgage as I would in the baseline scenario either, as my investment returns should be covering that.

Green = Baller level

Now, this green 'Baller' level is a crazy number. If you've still got a mortgage, then let's budget that in, and maybe work off $250,000 a year for your living expense number. If you think $250,000 is still too low, then customise this for whatever you reckon would make you feel like a baller.

Using my example, let's work this out being [$250,000 + $72,000 (mortgage)] divide by 0.08 and divide that by 0.75 for tax = **$5,366,666**.

So, in summary, my targets for invested assets would be:

Red level = $1,118,866 (Current living expenses paid for, and no mortgage covered)
Orange level = $3,152,200 (Extra $50,000 in living expenses versus current, plus mortgage repayments taken care of)
Green level = $5,366,666 ($250,000 in living expenses, plus mortgage repayments taken care of)

It's also worth noting that I believe superannuation counts when working towards these targets. So, if you already had $500,000 in super and $200,000 in invested assets outside of super, you would only need $418,866 more to reach the red baseline level.

This method is the best way I've come up with to calculate targets to reach financial freedom, as it does take into account your calculated living expenses, mortgage repayments, and your desired extra living expenses, in the orange and green levels.

But, as you can see, this is entirely dependent on people's personal circumstances and their desires. For instance, my parents' wealth is invested through superannuation and, because they are over 60 and retired, they pay no tax on their earnings in super. This means for their calculations, I would not need to adjust for tax.

Some clients might already have their house paid off. Therefore, there is no mortgage adjustment and it is all just covering levels of living expenses. Some clients might be perfectly happy living frugally, or they may have already amassed a decent amount of wealth. They may have already hit their red, orange, or even their green targets. I encourage you to work out what your numbers are for you and your family using a similar method to what I've suggested above.

Exercise: Calculate Your Magic Numbers

To assist with this exercise, I've put the table below to help contain all the different numbers. In the first table I've filled out my example which is the numbers mentioned above. The second table is empty for you to fill in.

My example (from numbers above):

Level	Living Expenses	Mortgage	Investment Return	Tax Rate	Invested Assets Required
Red	$67,132	n/a	0.08 (8%)	25%	$1,118,866
Orange	$67,132 + $50,000	$72,000	0.08 (8%)	25%	$3,152,200
Green	$250,000	$72,000	0.08 (8%)	25%	$5,366,666

Your numbers:

Level	Living Expenses	Mortgage	Investment Return	Tax Rate	Invested Assets Required
Red					
Orange					
Green					

What did you learn from your number?

What I discovered is my red number was a lot less than I thought it was going to be. There was a thought process when my parents were investing and planning for retirement that you needed at least $1,000,000 before you could even consider retiring, and I thought that was still not going to produce a great outcome. But seeing my red target gives me hope that that's very achievable, while still giving me a pretty decent lifestyle.

When I look at the orange and green numbers, they seem a little bit far to reach, but a lot closer than they would have 3, 4 or 5 years ago. The exciting thing is that, as a business owner, there is always a potential if you are building towards it, to *sell* your business.

If you were to do that, then the proceeds you earn would count towards your invested assets (assuming obviously that you invest them after the sale). If you are building your business for sale and it is already worth $1 or $2 million, then this can bring those red, orange, or green numbers a lot closer, sooner. I hope that was a fun process for you to go through, and it gives you the clarity and hope that you need to be able to make it a reality.

What Are Your Current Net Investable Assets?

The last thing I'd love you to do as part of this exercise is to calculate roughly what your net invested assets are right now. This will give you the ability to work out where you are at in comparison to your Red, Orange or Green targets.

I've put together a table below. It sets out the different classes of assets that you might have (and there's room for more if you have other types of assets).

In the first column there you've got **asset value**. This is the gross asset value before any debt attached to that. Then in the next column, you've got the debt amount and in the final column on the right, you've got the net asset position. Once you're done with the rows, then calculate the total net assets to give you your figure to compare to your Red, Orange, or Green targets above.

Just a note on the business value: A lot of people overestimate what their business is worth, or will they have an idea of "I wouldn't accept any less than $X million" to sell. I'd suggest that you keep your estimate of business value very reasonable here.

If you've got a rule of thumb valuation for your industry (for instance, a cents in the dollar of revenue, or a multiple of an easily determinable profit) then you could use that. But if you feel like it would be quite difficult to sell your business at least for any significant value, then I would not include a figure here, as it may be a struggle to turn your current business into cash.

If you'd like to learn more about this, in the book *Total Financial Control*, I explore guidelines and concepts around business value, including what we look for as accountants and how to grow your business to be able to eventually sell it for a decent amount.

Use the table on the following page to calculate a 'back of the napkin' current net invested assets.

	Asset Value	(Less Debt)	Net Asset
Cash		N/A	
Shares / Managed Funds			
Residential investment property			
Commercial property			
Business Sale Value			
Cryptocurrency			
Other invested assets:			
Super – Spouse A		N/A	
Super – Spouse B		N/A	
Total Net Invested Assets			

Bonus

If you are a client of Inspire, you may have already set up your Wealth Portal.

But if you are reading this, and would like to explore an online solution to keeping track of your family's net wealth, then please check out Inspire's Wealth Portal offering.

You can find more about it at https://inspire.accountants/wealth-for-life-resources

Our portal gives you the ability to track your wealth and, using a pro-subscription (free to all Inspire clients) it will update your bank balances and loan amounts, get information from RPData to update your estimated property values, track your vehicles' estimated value, track shares, portfolio and even superannuation values (through industry super or if you link in your SMSF value through our SMSF software).

There's plenty this stuff can do – and if you:

- Are a client, please check in with your accountant at Inspire to get this activated (if it's not already)

- Otherwise, if you are keen to sign up, you can get the free version by going to the Wealth for Life book resources page. Simply follow the steps to set up your account. If you'd like to explore a 'pro' subscription, then please reach out to us.

Part Summary

We've come to the end of the foundations for building Wealth for Life.

I hope this has given you reflection on how far you've already come in your wealth creation journey, and concepts for planning out the rest of your life, in general but also from a financial perspective (which is where advisers can come in and assist you).

I also trust that Step 3 gave you some tangible goals to target to reach financial freedom at its different levels. Fingers crossed that you are already a fair way along to hitting your red baseline target.

In Part 2, Steps 4 to 6 of the book, we are going to be talking about structures. This is where it gets technical in parts, when we talk about things like insurance, estate planning, and the power of superannuation.

I trust that you can bear with this next section even though it can be a bit meaty on technical information. If you master it, then you're going to set yourself up with some great structures to help you turbocharge your wealth creation journey, build a significant legacy and protect it from a downside as best you can.

Implementation Checklist

Step 1

Have you downloaded and completed the Bucket List?	☐
Have you set a date and booked your first Relationship Retreat?	☐

Step 2

Have you completed the 'Trim the Fat' exercise?	☐
Have you downloaded the Automated Household Budget spreadsheet and filled it out?	☐
Have you set up your multiple bank accounts?	☐
Have you set up your automatic transfers from your business account to your main personal, and then the automated transfers into each of your personal sub-accounts?	☐

Step 3

Have you calculated your Financial Freedom Magic Number?	☐
Have you calculated your Red, Orange, and Green targets for your Magic Number?	☐
Have you taken stock of your current net asset position?	☐
Have you set up your Inspire Wealth Portal account?	☐

PART 2: Structures

n Part 2, we will cover functional things to put in place, or consider, financially.

We'll get started in Step 4 by talking about putting a backup plan in place, by way of having insurance to protect you and your family against unexpected events that life might throw at you.

Then, we will talk about estate planning and why it is critically important for business owners to get right.

Finally, we will wrap up the Structures Part by talking about superannuation, and Self Managed Super Funds, in a lot of detail. SMSF's extremely useful for our small business clients, so I've spent a good amount of time making sure that I share the great benefits that an SMSF can give business owners.

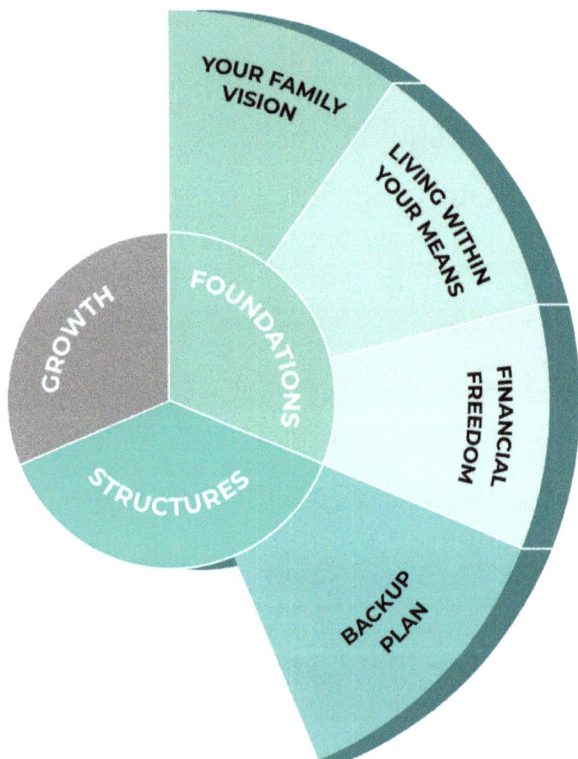

Step 4:
Backup Plan

*"Doesn't expecting the unexpected make
the unexpected expected?"*

Bob Dylan

One thing I think is *super* important that helps create immediate and long-term security for yourself and your family, is to always have a backup plan in place. This starts simply by asking yourself (in an almost morbid way), what could go wrong. This might sound like this:

- **"What if I got sick and I couldn't work for months?"**

- **"What if I passed away? How would my spouse or family keep a roof over their heads?"**

- **"What if I got diagnosed with cancer and I needed urgent expensive treatment?"**

If anything like the above was to happen, I personally wouldn't want to leave Stevie in a position where she would have to go back to full-time work to put food on the table, put Rose and any other of our children into full-time care, and struggle to make ends meet. I've sought out insurance to protect against as much of this as possible.

Below, I explore the different types of insurance that I've considered, as well as my thought process behind each one. Please keep in mind that I am not a financial adviser, and if you want to look into getting insurance for you and your family, then I recommend you seek out a qualified financial adviser who is experienced with insurance to assist you. Inspire can guide you to someone whom we have been working with for over a decade that helps me, my family, and our clients with insurance.– Just send an email to me at ben@inspire.accountants with the subject line: 'I need an insurance hero' and we'll connect you up.

Life Insurance (Death Insurance)

Life insurance (sometimes called death insurance) is paid out when you die. It's kind of an obvious one from the name and, from what I've seen, it's one of the most common insurances that people take out. Life insurance can sometimes be paid out when the insured person gets a terminal illness diagnosis (for instance, cancer) and has less than 12 months to live.

As I said earlier, I would always want my family to be taken care of if I passed away unexpectedly. On the contrary, if Stevie were to pass away, then I would also want some cover because I would want to step back from work to spend more time with the kids without affecting our overall income or lifestyle. So, we would also want the right level of cover for Stevie's life – not just mine. The way I look at it is to ask, "What would your loved ones need in order to continue living the life they are living, if you were to pass away?"

Life insurance can be paid out and then the beneficiaries will use it to pay debt or the mortgage. They can use it for living expenses or investment purposes (whatever they want, really).

Tips About Life Insurance

There are two main ways of owning life insurance. The first one is in your name, and you get the amount paid out to your estate or nominated beneficiaries in the event of your passing. Otherwise, the second option is to own and pay for it within your superannuation fund.

The insurance proceeds get paid to your superannuation fund and dealt with by the trustee of the fund according to the instructions you provided them on how your super should be dealt with on your passing. For more on this, please see the superannuation in *Step 5: Leave your Legacy.*

In my own calculation of how much insurance I would like for my life cover, I take into consideration:

- The amount to clear any debt on the home I'm living in

- Any other debt that has a non-liquid asset attached to it, such as credit cards, personal loans, or business debt (if the business is not readily saleable)

- Amounts to pay for living expenses for Stevie and any children we have, without her going back to work (this increases for each child we would have)

- Reduce these amounts by assets already invested (that are very liquid)

Here's an example of the table I use when I'm considering my own insurances. You will see there's a column for your notes as well.

You'll see 'assets to provide for living expenses' which is increased by $500,000 per child. The thought process is that this invested returning 5 – 8% should be plenty to put food on the table and the kids through school. (The mortgage is cleared in the first line, which is the current debt on the home.)

What to consider	Ben's numbers	Your notes
Current debt on my own home	1,000,000	
Other debt to clear	300,000	
No. of children u18 x $500,000	1,000,000	
Assets to provide for living expenses	1,000,000	
Less net assets already invested (not business)	(400,000)	
Total estimate of cover	2,900,000	

Also, I do believe there may be a point where people are self-insured. What I mean by this is they have enough assets to cover the requirements that they might need in an insurable event like death. For instance, if the above dot points added up to $3.3 million, but I had $4 million in investments, then I feel there would be limited reasons for me to need or take out a policy for life insurance.

In my calculation, I personally don't include to pay out debt that relates to investments such as an investment property or if we had margin loans, as the underlying asset could be sold if needed to pay the debt out without a significant lifestyle change.

TPD (Total & Permanent Disability)

TPD insurance stands for total and permanent disability insurance where you have had a permanent injury or illness, making it difficult or impossible to return to work. The idea of TPD insurance is to support you and your family's living costs and pay for medical and rehabilitation costs.

This can matter maybe even more important than life insurance because not only are you potentially unable able to work, but you are also very dependent on other people for help. You may want to think about some of the things that are covered in the life insurance part above such as:

- The amount to clear any debt on my own home that I'm living in

- Any other debt that has a non-liquid asset attached to it, such as credit cards, personal loans, or business debt (if the business is not readily saleable)

- Amounts to pay for living expenses for Stevie and any children we have, without her going back to work

But also, additional things including:

- Medical costs for your injury or illness

- Rehabilitation costs

- Adjustments to your home or work to allow you disabled access

- A home nurse or care

Tips About TPD

Each insurer has different definitions of what it means to be *totally and permanently disabled.*

You can also take out cover for either:

- **Your own occupation** – Which is the fact that you're unable to work again in the job you are working in before your disability. This cover is generally more expensive because it may be more likely to happen compared to 'any' occupation insurance. It is also usually only available outside of superannuation.

- **Any occupation** – This cover is if you are unable to work in any job suited to your education training or experience. So, if you are able to answer a phone and work in a call centre, even though you may be physically disabled, there is a chance that you may not be paid out because you could still work in **some form** of occupation.

As with any insurance policy, it is always best to be clear on the terms and conditions of the policy before taking out the cover.

Income Protection

Income protection insurance ordinarily covers you for up to 75% of your income in case you're not able to work. My policy covers me for 75% of my income and I keep getting it updated and reviewed as I earn more or increase business profits from Inspire.

A lot of people will insure their car without question, or their home, but often people find it surprisingly more effort to decide when it comes to insuring their income stream from working.

I've had many chats with my friend and financial planner Nick Webb about this exact thing. I personally am not keen to take the risk of having no income protection insurance when it could mean a huge change in lifestyle if I went without cover because something happened to me.

So, if you're in a position where you're insuring the car or your house which are the assets that your income produces, then I would encourage you to very strongly consider income protection insurance, if you haven't taken it out already.

Tips About Income Protection

Please watch out for the 'waiting period' on your insurance cover. This is the time that you're unable to work before your policy starts paying out and replacing your income. These are often anywhere between 30, 60 or 90 days of waiting periods.

For instance, a 30-day waiting period means you need to be sick for over 30 days and unable to work before the policy kicks in and starts replacing your income. Just think back to the last time you were sick for over a month and unable to work. Thankfully, for me, that's never happened, but if it did, then it sounds like quite a serious illness.

Also, when you are choosing a waiting period, consider if you have a cash buffer or cash reserve available to use first, before you need the insurance to kick in. For instance, if you've got three months of living expenses tucked away in a savings account, that's 90 days' worth of expenses sorted for you and your family. This means you might be very okay having a 90-day waiting period before insurance starts replacing your income.

The longer the waiting period that you choose, the cheaper the insurance generally is, because the less risk it is to the insurer of you getting sick for that long period of time. As an example, there are many more illnesses that might knock you out for a month than illnesses that could knock you out for over three months. Therefore, there is less risk to the insurer, and less likely to pay, which means a little bit cheaper usually for your policy compared to a policy with a shorter waiting period.

Also, for self-employed people, income protection insurance is a little trickier than providing payslips when you go for cover and, at the time of claim, have to prove your income. It's best to work with a financial adviser who can not only talk you through the insurance cover requirements and recommendations but also who works as a broker with the insurance companies to find the best insurer that matches your circumstances. They will take your income documents, such as your tax returns and financial statements, and work with insurers to get the best outcome for you.

Also, keep in mind that at the time of claim, you may be required to show your current income. I've seen it happen in the past with a client that they took out income protection insurance when they were being paid a salary of a high amount (roughly $200,000) before they started their business.

They had an accident and claimed their insurance after they had started their business. As the business was in the first couple of years of trading, there was a lot of re-investment into the business, therefore the income was relatively low. They were only able to show around $40,000 of taxable income on tax returns and unfortunately insurers pay them 75% of what they were able to prove, even though they were paying the insurance premiums based on earning a $200,000 salary. The lesson here is to make sure that you regularly review your insurance as your income level or employment circumstances may change.

One added benefit of Income Protection is that if owned in your own name personally, the insurance premiums your pay are 100% tax deductible to you.

Trauma/Critical Illness

In addition to Medicare and private health insurance, you can also get insurance cover for severe accidents or illnesses. This is sometimes called trauma insurance or critical illness cover.

These are commonly for big health issues such as heart-related illnesses or cancer. Different insurers cover different things so please double-check what you're covered for to make sure you're not assuming that you are. This type of insurance can cover emergency medical treatment such as out-of-pocket expenses when it comes to treating heart attacks or cancer. It's also intended to cover things like the cost of therapy, nursing care, or special transport required as a result of your illness.

Tips About Trauma/Critical Illness Insurance

We also had a client who mentioned they had a Melanoma removed during their skin check appointment. Again, having worked with Nick Webb together for years, I heard that some insurers cover certain types of melanomas that trigger a pay-out of critical illness insurance.

I asked the client to reach out to their insurer to see if what was cut out was severe enough to trigger a claim. A few weeks later, that client had $40,000 paid in their account from their insurer.

Overall Insurance Things To Keep In Mind

There are a handful of things to know when you are considering different types of insurance.

Stepped or level premiums

This relates to the increasing cost of insurance as both you and the policy ages. Generally, the two options are stepped premiums or level premiums.

- **Stepped premiums** - These premiums are recalculated that each policy renewal, and usually increase each year based on the higher chance of a claim as you age

- **Level premiums** - These are usually billed with a higher premium at the start of the policy, but the increase in cost isn't based on your age, so the increases are usually slower over time

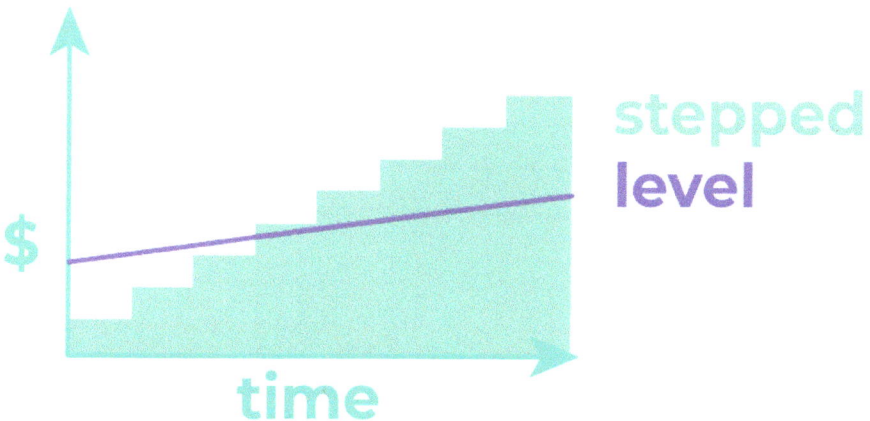

My own thought process is that I plan on becoming self-insured relatively quickly and reducing my level of cover as I go. So, I'm taking the bet that stepped premiums may work out better for me if I don't need insurance in five to ten years. If you plan on holding insurance for a long time, level premiums may end up being more cost-effective.

Waiting periods before you can claim

I had a friend who soon after they took out insurance ended up having cancer. Unfortunately, the diagnosis was within the 90-day waiting period from the time they took out cover to when they were covered for cancer. They were not able to claim on the policy. Therefore, keep in mind that your insurance may have a waiting period before you can claim, so, please ask the question if it's important to you.

The application process

As part of most insurance application processes, you will need to tell the insurer anything that could affect their decision to provide you with that insurance. This information can also be required to be provided even if you renew or change your insurance.

This can include things like:

- **Your age**

- **Your job and employment status**

- **Your medical history**

- Your family history of diseases

- Things that are in your lifestyle, such as smoking or drugs

- High-risk sports or hobbies, such as skydiving

If an insurer doesn't ask you for your medical history, you may have exclusions on the policy or a narrower cover than if you do go through a full application process. This may also apply if you have default cover through your superannuation fund. This gives you all the more reason to do a full insurance review with a qualified financial adviser who knows their way around personal insurance.

Challenges getting cover

I've seen with some clients that their occupation or their previous health history has prevented them from getting certain types of cover. The insurer looks at their level of risk with that person and, for instance, if they've previously been diagnosed with cancer and are in remission, they still might have a seriously high chance of developing a critical illness because of their previous cancer diagnosis.

Also, some insurers look to insure certain types of occupation that have a high health risk including mental health risks. For instance, I've seen air traffic controllers struggle to get any insurance because of their occupation. In these instances, if you've had previous health conditions or you're in a high-risk occupation, please reach out to an insurance expert to double check that there's not an insurer who may cover you.

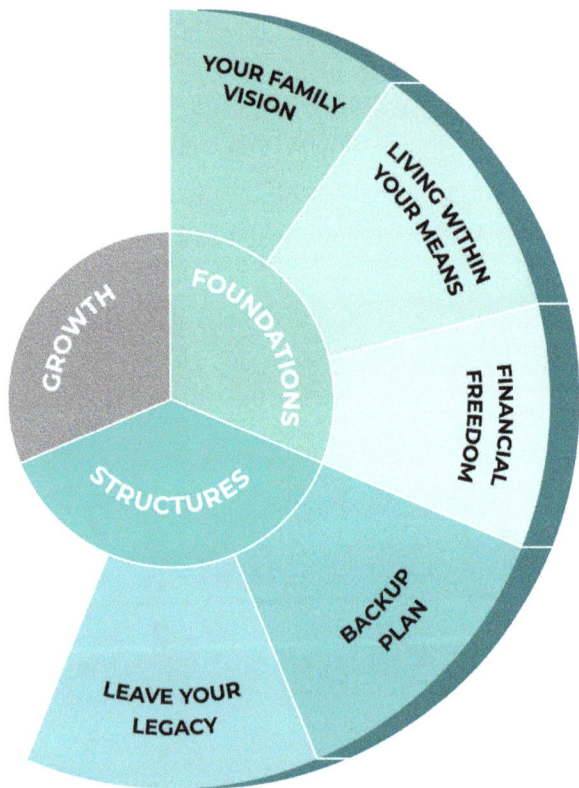

Step 5:
Leave Your Legacy

"The greatest legacy one can pass on to one's children and grandchildren is not money or other material things accumulated in one's life, but rather a legacy of character and faith."

Billy Graham

The purpose of this step is to talk about your estate planning. To me, estate planning is the process of documenting the specific instructions, both legally and morally binding, on how your various assets and entities are dealt with when you can't do it yourself: if you've either lost the capacity or you pass away.

Depending on the statistic that you read, around 60% of Australians die without having a Will.

A couple of bad situations that relate to this I've seen in my life one was when I was younger. I had a good friend whose dad passed away without a Will. He had a bit of wealth and property and two sons, one of them being my friend.

Unfortunately, when he passed, he had no Will, and his son stepped up and helped to sort out his affairs. It was extremely difficult to get anything done because there was no Will. It took months to even coordinate and make decisions, and I think it stretched out a good 12 to 18 months to wrap up what would and could have been a relatively simple estate.

While no one was relying on any income from the rental properties he had, or living in the house where he lived, I just remember being surprised at how simple it should have been and how frustrated my friend was that his father didn't have a Will. It would have made it a lot simpler to get through the process. That, on top of the grief of losing his dad, was pretty rough.

The other thing I want to mention is that I've also seen a Will that did not match the person's wealth or family circumstances. I've seen this situation where a person passed away with a cheap three or four-page will for an estate that was worth millions of dollars. It had a likely potential of being contested, due to family not getting along.

This person had companies, trusts, and a self-managed super fund, and they were a business owner. From my perspective, the three or four pages would not cut it when it came to having a strong estate plan in place.

So, from these two stories I want to ask you:

1. **Do you have an up-to-date will?**

2. And by "up-to-date" do you remember generally what's happening, and who is in control if you pass away?

3. If your Will is likely to get contested, do you have measures in place to reduce this risk, or to make it not worthwhile?

4. Do you have documents in place that detail who the control passes to for your trusts and companies and self-managed super fund?

5. Have you considered the tax outcome of passing your family wealth onto the next generation?

It is vital to answer and set in place the right estate to address all of the above questions.

An Estate Plan Is More Than Just A Will

It's important for me to say as we transition into the detailed stuff shortly, that, as a business owner, an estate plan is not just simply having a Will done. When you have advanced structures like companies, trusts, and self-managed super funds, there is much more to consider when you are planning to pass on your wealth to future generations.

Different Documents For Different Assets

In the table below, I have outlined the type of names or structures that you might own assets in the left column. In the right column, I've outlined the document required to deal with the assets that are held in that entity or name.

Assets held in	Document Required
Personal name	Will
Joint names (joint tenants)	None - survivor
Companies	See shareholders
Trusts (Discretionary)	See trust deed
Superannuation	Nominations
Insurance pay outs	Policy Owner

You can pretty quickly see that having a Will only deals with assets in your name. It can usually have a role to play in how the other documents operate and how the tax plays out for your estate. Shortly, I'll go through a high-level overview of each of those key documents, what's in them, and what you need to think about.

Key Documents For Estate Planning

Your Will

Your Will maps out the key people involved in your estate plan. The three main questions it answers is:

- **Who controls your estate (the 'executor')?**

- **Where do you want your estate to go (the 'beneficiaries')?**

- **The method of how it goes to the beneficiaries (directly or via a testamentary trust)?**

Your Will deals with assets in your name such as your bank accounts, property in your name, and personal assets such as cars, furniture, jewellery, and heirlooms.

Note: If you are the risk-taker, then when we structure your assets and businesses from an asset protection perspective, you will likely have very limited assets in your own personal name. Most of your wealth would likely be held in trusts, companies, or super. There is a section coming up in the book on dealing with assets in those entities, but that may be the more critical part of your estate plan, namely how the control passes from those entities.

Who's your executor?

One of the first questions to answer is who controls your estate, or more specifically: Who is your executor?

The role of the executor in your Will is someone who carries out your wishes after you have passed away. They need to pay all your debts as well as any tax that's owing before distributing the estate or remaining assets to your beneficiaries (as you've specified in your Will).

Some of the things the executor is responsible for include:

- **They need to locate your final will. It is best to let them know where it is and maybe give them a copy**

- **They're responsible for dealing with the Funeral Home and dealing with your body (e.g. cremation, burial)**

- **They apply for your death certificate**

- **They obtain probate, if required**

- **They work out what your assets and liabilities are**

- **They pay any outstanding debts and expenses of your estate**

- **They pay the remaining assets to your beneficiaries**

The person you choose as your executor doesn't have to act without any help. They can engage advisers to help them through the process.

What we normally see here is that people choose their spouse as an initial executor. The great thing though, is that you can list more than one executor if your first choice isn't alive, or if they cannot act as your executor at the time, for some other reason.

So, after your spouse is listed as the initial executor, we often see parents as the next best bet. If not that, then a trusted brother or sister, or even a close friend. You can also nominate an executor from each family if you have a spouse. So, for instance, one of your brothers and your brother-in-law might be listed as joint executors and they will be required to make the decisions together.

You can nominate as many levels of executors as you like in your Will. For example, you could have your initial executor, then your first backup, then your second backup, then your third backup, and so on. We don't normally see Wills with more than a third backup, which means that three levels of an executor must either pass away or not be able to act, before that third backup is required to be the executor.

Another thing that lawyers often like to see is having mirror Wills. This means you have two spouses where the people that they nominate as executor and backup executors are exactly the same in both Wills.

The reason why the lawyers often want these mirror Wills is for cases where there is an unwanted different outcome for the executor role, based on the timing of death or incapacity. An example of this might be if both spouses are in a car accident and one dies two hours after the first spouse passes away, then the executor role may be completely different if they are not listed as exactly the same in both Wills.

I understand that the decision here can be pretty tough. The executor has a key role to play in your estate plan. A tip that might help – and what we often see is where we use these people, in the order that you specify them as your executor, for other roles as well. This means that the executors will also be listed as the power of attorney or for backup roles of control in your companies and trusts.

Who are your Beneficiaries?

Who will receive your estate?

Answering this question may be very straightforward in most cases. But, if you don't have children, you have a blended family or an intense or complicated family situation, then it can prove to be a bit tricky.

Ordinarily what most people do is list their spouse as the first beneficiary to receive everything – 100% of their estate. Then, if the spouse is not around to receive the estate (because they too have passed away, for example), it generally falls back to the children and/or the grandchildren.

'Gift over' provision

The other thing we need to think about with beneficiaries is the concept called the 'gift over' provision. This generally means that if the person you specify to receive your estate passes away and you choose to have the *gift over provision* applying to their gift, then their gift will go to their children. If you choose for the gift over provision to NOT apply, then their intended gift will return back to the net estate, if they have passed away by the time you die and reallocated to the remaining beneficiaries.

Specific Gifts

You can also list specific gifts if you would like jewellery, heirlooms, or certain items to be left for a certain beneficiary in particular. We can also use specific gifts in the case where we want shares in certain companies or units in trusts to end up with a specific person.

Calamity Event

The other thing you can specify is what happens in a 'calamity event'. This is if all your listed beneficiaries (ordinarily your spouse, children, and their children) are not alive when you pass away. This is an awful thing to think about, but it is best to have an answer to pop into your Will.

We often see things like where the estate is passed on to each of the spouses' parents in equal parts. Or, in another example, the estate might then be left to brothers and sisters of the spouses in equal parts, or on equal sides of the family. I have even seen the estate being left to certain charities in a calamity event, which you also can specify in your Will.

Testamentary Trusts

There are generally two ways that you can pass assets from your personal name / your estate to your beneficiaries.

The first way that lawyers generally refer to is the 'I love you' method, which is to pass assets from your estate directly into their name. We deal with a lot of business owners where estate planning requires us to think about asset protection, and for several reasons, we don't like assets going into personal names when there are better alternatives, especially on death.

The alternative method is to put the assets from the estate into a testamentary trust directly without them going into anyone's personal name. A testamentary trust operates in a similar way to a discretionary trust. There is a trustee who controls the trust. You can outline a principal or appointor or whose role is to hire and fire the trustee, and there are a set of beneficiaries as well.

So, instead of passing assets into the person's own name, the assets go into the testamentary trust so that you have that layer of separation between the assets and the beneficiary. This is for asset protection reasons.

Asset protection can protect against business risk, as well as potentially protect against beneficiaries' future spouses. In the case of younger children, or children where their inheritance is probably not best left to their own devices just yet, you can separate the role of the trustee (controller) and the beneficiary (who the assets should benefit).

The reason we would like to do this is that the child may not be able to or might be too young to make decisions for themselves, and we want someone trusted as the trustee to make decisions on their behalf. Remember that you can always change the trustee later once that child can be responsible for their own inheritance.

Memo of Directions (Letter of Wishes)

The next document I'd like to run through that is usually prepared when we take a client through the estate planning process is the memorandum ('memo') of directions. This is sometimes called the 'letter of wishes'.

This is not a legally binding letter, but is a set of instructions that the person who is passing away intends to leave to the people behind to help with the administration of their estate. This is different to the Will which *is* a legally binding document. To compare the two, some people will say the memo of directions is morally binding.

The purpose is to help the executor to make decisions about how the estate administration is handled or even things like where the kids will go to school. Even if the person hasn't passed away, but they've lost their capacity to function, you can include instructions about where that person wants to be looked after in care.

Some of the things which you may include in a memo of directions are:

- Specific instructions around how assets are used

- Why the Will says that certain beneficiaries get certain things and others didn't

- What age the kids should be before they receive direct access to their inheritance

- How to deal with collectable items and any information that may be required in order to deal with or sell them

- Where the pets go

- Funeral preferences such as burial vs cremation, if you have prepaid expenses etc.

- Directions around organ donation (although these should also be registered with the relevant government organisation as it may be too late to donate organs if it is only mentioned in the memo of directions). You can add yourself to the Register here https://donatelife.gov.au/

- Whom to notify once you've passed away

- Key contacts for advice such as accountants, lawyers, or financial planners

- What you would like done with your social media accounts

- Any contacts or details for digital assets

- Investment directions, such as what to hold or sell

- Details of your entities or structures, such as companies or trusts, and what to do with each

- Any insurance arrangements that you have

- Passwords, bank deposit boxes, or other information with third parties

Your memorandum of directions can be updated at any time without any witnesses or lawyers involved. Given the nature that it is only morally binding and not legally binding, keep in mind that any changes may not actually turn into reality. Depending on what you want to change, it may be better to do that as an update of your current Will instead.

Enduring Power of Attorney

The next document is called the enduring power of attorney.

These are different in each state or territory in Australia, so there may be small changes between each state on how this is organised and completed. For instance, there are different forms for each state.

A power of attorney deals with financial and health matters when the person has not passed away but they have lost the capacity to act for themselves. Alternatively, it can be activated on some other certain condition that you specify.

What I mean by that is, for instance, you can enact a power of attorney if you are going overseas. As an example, you might be in the middle of selling a property and you need someone to sign on your behalf. You can give that permission to the power of attorney to sign on your behalf while you're away.

This means that you can also set the power of attorney for a certain period of time, or for only a restricted amount of power, to deal with a limited situation. But in the context of estate planning, it is more related to a loss of capacity in the event where you do deteriorate mentally and you need others to act on your behalf.

You can assign different people to act for your health matters versus your financial matters, but most people have the same attorneys for health and financial matters.

We often look to the list of executors that a client prepared in the Will preparation stage for suggestions of who the power of attorneys might be.

You can also have more than one person appointed as a power of attorney. You can choose to have multiple people appointed severally, which means that any one of your attorneys may decide and sign, or you can appoint them jointly where they must all agree on the decisions. The other alternative is a majority – as in more than half of the assigned attorneys – must agree on the decisions.

There are some things that the lawyers will often suggest that go in the power of attorney that makes administration a little bit easier for the people in charge. This is because it's not a simple form, and banks and government don't take these power of attorneys lightly. This makes sense because you're literally giving the attorney the same power to act in your right as you have to act on your own behalf.

Dealing With Assets In The Following Entities

The next section is discussing what you need to consider if you have assets in other entities apart from your own name.

Companies

The first one is if you have assets held in companies.

Sometimes clients invest directly in their bucket company, or their trading entity is a company that has value. This can mean significant assets in companies that we need to deal with and how this portion of their wealth is passed on according to their wishes.

Now, the owners of companies are the company's shareholders. The shareholders control who the directors of the company are, and they have the ultimate control of the company. Often when we set structures up at Inspire, we will have a trust that owns the company. We do this for both asset protection and tax planning reasons. But sometimes, we see companies owned by the individual in their own right.

If the shares are owned in the person's name, then the Will determines where the shares go: either into a testamentary trust or directly to a beneficiary, which we spoke about earlier. Then that testamentary trust or beneficiary will control the company and, therefore, the company's assets or investments.

So, if the shares are held in individual names, we want to be mindful of which beneficiary or trust that goes to. In this case, you may want to do a specific gift rather than leave it in the net estate, if you want a specific outcome. If the shares in the company are held by a discretionary trust, please refer to the next section on who gets control of a trust.

Trusts

TRUST

The next entity we'll run through is for assets that are held in discretionary trusts.

Just a side note on unit trusts before we get into discretionary trusts. Unit trusts are generally a fixed entitlement to the trust and the assets of the trust. So, if you do have a unit trust, then please use the same thought process as the 'shares in a company' section above. Now, back to discretionary trusts.

There are a couple of key roles in a discretionary trust:

- **The trustee** - Who controls the day-to-day decisions and running of the trust

- **The appointor or principal** - Who has the ultimate control of the trust and can hire and fire the trustee

- **The beneficiaries** - These are the people for whom the trust was set up as beneficiaries

When we look at estate planning where assets are held in trusts, we want to look at the trust deed and what it says about the trustee and appointor / principal roles when those people pass away or lose the capacity to undertake that role.

The appointor or principal role is the key one, because it has the ultimate control of the trust.

In most deeds that we read, if the current appointor / principal passes away, then the control goes to their legal personal representative – also known as the executor listed in their Will. The trouble here is that they may not be your intended beneficiary of the trust assets, so please consider this. (As an example, let's say that your sister is the executor, but you want your children to end up with the trust assets. Then you will need some guidance for your sister to hold those trust assets for your children.)

Also, you may have a trust deed that says something completely different, so every trust deed needs to be read and clearly understood. It's best for a lawyer to do this. In the case that the appointor / principal succeeding you is not ideal for that role any more, you can prepare a deed of variation to the trust to specify who, and the order of who, should replace the appointor / principal if the current appointor / principal were to pass away, lose capacity, or other trigger events.

Wrapping up, the trust deed is important when looking at how assets that are held in a trust are passed to your intended beneficiaries.

Superannuation

The last entity I would like to cover is assets held in superannuation.

SMSF

It's important to make sure that you've got this one covered. Even if you are young and you don't have much super yet, depending on how your life insurance is structured, your super fund may receive your life insurance pay-out. This can end up being a substantial asset.

The way of ensuring an outcome, for where your super goes, is by putting in place a 'binding death benefit nomination' or what we refer to as a 'BDBN'. This binds the trustee of your super fund to pay your superannuation as per the instructions you have detailed in your BDBN.

You can nominate a particular person. For instance, directly to your spouse or a child. In this case, this superannuation amount skips your estate (and the potential for your superannuation amount to be contested in your estate) and must be paid straight to the person you have nominated.

This is great if your estate has a higher chance of being contested. The downside of this is if your super skips your personal estate and your Will, your super assets can't be passed onto your beneficiaries via a testamentary trust. Even though that is the case, we can look at things such as a superannuation proceeds trust instead.

Otherwise, you can make your nominated beneficiary of the BDBN for your estate to be dealt with under your Will. This is very common for clients where their estate has a very low risk of being contested.

Another option to consider, if you are paying a pension from your super fund, is to set up a reversionary pension. This means that on your passing; your pension reverts to your beneficiary listed in the pension documents and they start receiving your pension instead of you. This can have good tax outcomes as well, because your super remains in a pension state.

If no nominations are made for who your death benefits go to, then the trustee of your super fund will decide who receives your death benefit. This is hardly ever a great outcome, especially if you do not have a self-managed super fund and a third-party provider is making these decisions.

Life Insurance

I think it is worth mentioning about life insurance here as well. It's not quite an entity of its own, but it can be a large amount of money that is received by you or a related entity.

It's just a quick one to cover, but your 'policy holder' as listed on the insurance policy will be the person or entity receiving the pay-out of your life insurance. If your name is listed as the policyholder, the proceeds will be paid to your estate and be dealt with under your Will.

If it is your self-managed super fund or your superannuation account with another provider, then they will receive your life insurance proceeds and it will be dealt with how your superannuation nominations are stated.

Other Things To Consider

There are a few other things it is important for you to consider. Having taken many clients through the estate planning process together with lawyers, there are a couple of circumstances that can make estate planning difficult or where it adds complexity.

From my experience, the ones that come to mind are:

- If you've had children with previous partners
- If you've got an estranged relationship with any of your children
- It may be argued you don't have the mental capacity to sign a new Will or power of attorney
- If you have a blended family
- If you've got beneficiaries overseas
- If your executors or key people in your Will live overseas
- If you have limited family

Regardless of whether you've got tricky things going on or if your estate planning seems simple on the surface, the best thing to do is talk to someone who can guide you through the process and who has experience with estate planning specifically for business owners. You don't want to end up without a Will, or with a three- or four-page Will as a business owner when you pass away. So, if you haven't got these things in place, please make a note to do it soon.

Business Succession Planning

The topic of business succession planning is important to mention. This includes who the business and associated income and value go to, depending on how the business is structured (whether it's a company or a trust). You can refer to the earlier sections in the book on how each of those two entities is dealt with.

But the topic of business succession planning specifically relates more to the 'how it is to be done', from a management perspective rather than a legal perspective. For instance, if you are the key person in your business, here are some questions to answer in a business succession plan document:

- **Who will take the helm and physically run the business?**
- **Will it be your spouse?**
- **Or will it be a key team member or leader in the business?**
- **Will the business be sold soon after you pass?**
- **Or does the business have the ability to keep trading after you have passed away?**

- **How will the bills of the business be paid, or payroll met?**

These are the type of things that need to be thought about in a business succession plan where you've lost capacity or if you pass away. If this sounds like something you need or would like to do, we have a template we can share with you that runs through some of these questions and more.

Estate Planning Is Not Set & Forget

Once you have completed your estate plan, it's not something that is just set and forget.

There are a number of reasons why I suggest reviewing your estate plan regularly, which are:

- **If you get married or enter a de facto relationship** – This can cancel any previous Wills that you've created, and you'll need to adjust your documents to make sure your other estate planning documents fall into line with your new relationship.

- If you get divorced or end a de facto relationship – It would be ideal to quickly update your estate planning documents so that your ex partner doesn't end up with all your assets.

- **If you have children or grandchildren** - It doesn't necessarily mean that you need to redo your estate planning documents, but it's a good time to check that your documents in existence consider your children or grandchildren in the way that you want them to.

- **If you get seriously sick or have a terminal illness** – Ideally, you don't want to wait until this happens to get a Will, but again, it's another good time to review that your documents still make sense.

- **If you're about to go on an extended overseas holiday** - It's a good time to check, but also on your power of attorneys as well; as in certain situations these people can sign documents while you're away if needed such as selling a house on your behalf while you were gone.

- **If you have a significant change in wealth** that occured since you created your estate planning documents in the first place, such as a large increase in property value, business profit, you receive an inheritance etc.

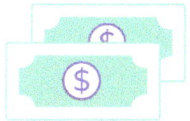

- **If you create companies or trusts or set up a self-managed super fund** - The goal is to make sure the set-up of these things is in alignment with your other estate planning documents.

COMPANY **TRUST** **SMSF**

- A key person such as your executor or beneficiary passes away or loses capacity.

And the last one is that time passes - and I recommend reviewing at least every three years (maximum), but as regular as an annual review.

Estate Planning Exercise: 1 Page Estate Plan

One of the exercises I get clients to do is to fill out is a bit of a brief or form including some general questions about their estate planning.

Below, I have detailed what I call the *one-page estate plan*. It asks high-level questions about your estate plan wishes that can be used to guide conversations with lawyers around the drafting of your key documents. Please note that it is not intended to replace a Will, but rather to help in the process of getting your estate planning done.

Have a go at filling out the below if you're keen to do so, and then work either with us or with a good adviser to complete your estate planning.

Executors: Who controls my Estate?

First Preference	First Backup	Second Backup

Beneficiaries: Who receives my Estate?

To Whom	Proportion ($ or % or Equal Shares)	Via Testamentary Trust?	Gift over Applying?

If those people have passed away, who do you want it to go to then?

Where do my superannuation payments go to?

How are Company & Trust assets to be dealt with?

Power of Attorney

First Attorney	Backup Attorney

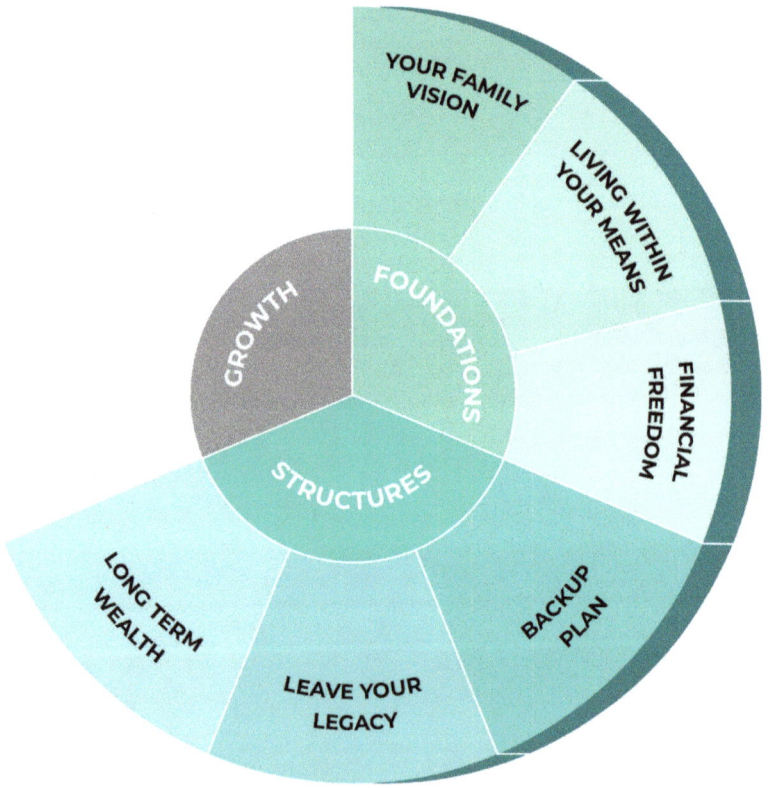

GROWTH

FOUNDATIONS

STRUCTURES

YOUR FAMILY VISION

LIVING WITHIN YOUR MEANS

FINANCIAL FREEDOM

BACKUP PLAN

LEAVE YOUR LEGACY

LONG TERM WEALTH

Step 6:
Long Term Wealth

"The question isn't at what age I want to retire,
it's at what income."

George Foreman

have had a love for SMSF's ever since I first started in accounting.

SMSF is an acronym that stands for a **Self-Managed Superannuation Fund**. It is an option for you to directly manage your own superannuation through your own entity that you set up and are the trustee of. This is compared with typical industry or corporate super funds where this is delegated to a business who manages your super along with a pool of other people's superannuation money.

In my first year of working in accounting, when I was straight out of school, I was auditing SMSF's at KPMG and learning about the rules of SMSFs. In 2010, when I changed employers, I went from auditing dozens of funds every year, to preparing the tax compliance and administration for every fund that the firm looked after. In 2011, I set up a self-managed super fund with my parents which gave me hands-on experience as a member of a fund. It taught me the complexities involved when preparing investment strategies, even things like my parents taking pensions from the fund as well.

I saw everything from basic simple funds that were invested in shares and cash, right through to some crazy investments in famous porn posters (you read that right – very strange), and even a fund where the member had sold a business, paid a huge chunk of cash into his fund, and had been living out of his fund to put food on the table and pay his mortgage. Oh dear!

Around about 28% of our clients at inspire have an SMSF and I have advised hundreds of trustees over the years in things such as:

- Carrying out property development;
- Fund businesses;
- Investing in private companies;
- Angel investing;
- Purchasing commercial property;
- Purchasing residential property;
- Borrowing money from banks;
- Borrowing money from related parties;
- Paying no tax on massive capital gains;

all using self-managed super funds.

On a national level, there were about 70 SMSFs set up every single day in 2021, and I feel more Australians are seeing the benefits and freedoms that SMSFs give. On 30 June 2021 there were 597,900 SMSF's in Australia, with 1,114,529 members – that's about 1 in every 23 Australians.

There are plenty of reasons why we love them, which I'll go through in this step. Eight of the main benefits are:

1. Engagement with your super

2. Family fund

3. Control tax

4. Investment strategy

5. Leverage

6. Insurance

7. Incapacity planning

8. Estate planning

Engagement With Your Super

The difference between SMSF vs. Corporate Super Funds

One of the first things I talk about when discussing engagement with a client is the differences between a self-managed super fund versus their current corporate or industry super fund. The first thing here is that one of the differences is in the name. The industry or corporate super fund will manage your super for you, whereas you need to manage your SMSF yourself.

Another thing that we find with members of SMSFs is that they are more engaged with how much super they have, how much it is earning, where it is invested, and what their targets or goals are with it. We often see them involving their SMSF in their business if they run a business. For instance, by buying a commercial property that their business rents from their SMSF.

I strongly believe that self-managing your super gives you a much stronger connection to your super and your overall wealth creation journey.

Comparing the costs

The other question that I am often asked by clients is what the differences in costs are for running an SMSF versus a corporate or industry super fund.

An industry or corporate super fund generally charges a **percentage-based fee** on the balance of your superannuation, while an SMSF usually has **fixed administration and compliance costs** associated with it.

Break Even

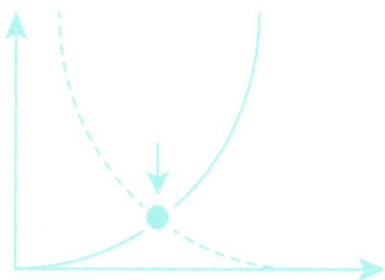

There will be a break-even point. To work that out, you'll need to have a look at the current fees that you're paying in your industry super fund and compare that with the relatively fixed costs of running your SMSF.

For instance, if you are paying 1.5% in total fees and have a balance of $200,000 in your super, then you will be paying $3,000 in fees each year. This is compared to say an SMSF, where the total running costs of your SMSF might be priced at $3,000 while your balance is anywhere up to $500,000.

If these are your numbers, then your breakeven point for the SMSF is $200,000. (Note: this excludes setup costs for the SMSF, which can be a few thousand in any case.)

Regardless, costs are only one thing to consider when setting up an SMSF and are usually not a top priority for clients. It is the other things that you can do with your super fund that make the decision to switch to a SMSF a no-brainer.

How much do you need in super to set one up?

One of the most popular questions when it comes to SMSF's is, "How much do I need to set one up?" If you were to Google this question, then the most common answer that would pop up is anywhere between $200,000 and $250,000.

Now keep in mind that this is usually referring to the fund as a total, rather than each member on their own. So, if you have a husband and wife with $125,000 each in super, that would combine together to give a $250,000 fund.

Now, the costs of an SMSF are usually one of the main things to consider which we've gone into a bit of detail in the previous section – the breakeven point of fees is usually the discussion. My opinion is that costs aren't the 'be all and end all' of an SMSF, and while I would strongly question why someone would set up a fund with $50,000 in their super, there is no legal minimum you need to set one up.

I believe that there are other benefits people look at with SMSF's, and the costs are secondary considerations. These benefits are usually to do with limitations of other industry funds which you can do in SMSF, such as:

- To invest in direct residential or commercial property

- To loan money for the purchase of certain investments (most commonly, for residential and commercial property)

- To access non-listed investments

- To invest in physical holdings of precious metals

- The ability for the SMSF to pay for learning in conferences around superannuation for the trustees

- The ability to pool money with other non-related super funds to make large investments in businesses or property development

- Not having to lodge a form with a third-party super provider (for whatever reason) and wait days or weeks for a response

- Flexibility in how and when you draw your pension throughout the year

- A combination of any of the above, and more!

At the end of the day, I feel like how much you need in super to warrant an SMSF is highly dependent on what your intentions are to do with it, and the cost should be considered relative to those intentions.

The 'SM' in 'SMSF'

I just wanted to pop in a final reminder and a bit of a warning that the 'SM' in 'SMSF' means **self-managed**. This means that it requires diligence to set up and run the fund. It has compliance requirements and rules of the game that you need to abide by so that you don't breach the superannuation rules, which can have quite large penalties if broken. There is also an annual audit required by a third-party auditor which, as accountants, we can organise on your behalf. Their role is to make sure that you haven't breached the Superannuation Act and that your reports are accurate.

If you are working with a good accountant, then this process is easy and staying within the rules is as simple as asking the question when one pops up. I have seen quite a few sticky situations where the trustees have knowingly or unknowingly breached the rules or had questionable advice and we've had to dig them back out of a hole. The best thing to do is work with someone who knows the boundaries from the start and who helps you work within them, while leveraging the power of an SMSF.

Family Fund

Another benefit of an SMSF is that you can involve your family.

For many years, the limit of the number of people in an SMSF was four, but as of 1 July 2021 you can have up to six members in your SMSF. More is not necessarily better though, and the statistics show that only 7% have funds that have three or more members as of 30 June 2021.

There are complications when you have more than perhaps one or two members. The most obvious of these is that you will need to make decisions together, if you are all directors or trustees. I usually talk about the three 'D's when it comes to having multiple members in a fund that can make things a bit hairy.

Up to 6 members (as of 1 July 2021)

Death

When someone passes away, generally that balance needs to be paid out of the fund in cash, either to a person or maybe to their estate. This means that assets might need to be liquidated. But, if the assets are things such as property, and that property has some significance to the remaining members, then it may be very difficult or frustrating to have to sell that property to pay out the death benefits.

Disability

Another thing to think about when we talk about disability is, for example, when the main members, being you or your spouse, are disabled and unable to run the SMSF. This would then need either your power of attorney or the other members of your super fund to act on your behalf. This could complicate things or cause undesirable outcomes for you if it is not carefully planned.

Divorce

The other situation that can make an SMSF tricky is the situation of a divorce.

I'll give two examples. The first one is your own divorce, where you might only have two members in the fund and you will likely you need to split one member out and leave one member in. You may need to sell assets to do this. This could be undesirable and the spouse has to agree, given they are likely a director of the trustee company or a trustee in their own right.

The second example is where you've got four members in the fund where you've brought in one of your children and their partner. If your child goes through a divorce, now you've got say three aligned members in the fund and one member who you'd like to manage out of the fund. This can be frustrating, as they have to agree to certain things, and if they're not willing to do something then that can make life pretty difficult for the management of the SMSF.

There is a solution to maintaining control of an SMSF in this sort of situation: by setting up a certain type of SMSF called a 'leading member' fund. If this situation is a concern and you would like more than you and your spouse in your fund, then please reach out and we can help to guide you through the process.

Control Tax

Another benefit of superannuation, in general, is to be able to control your tax outcomes.

The first thing that I like mentioning is that an SMSF or superannuation is a very low tax environment compared to other things, like companies or individuals. You will see this in the table below comparing different entities.

	INDIVIDUAL	COMPANY	TRUST	SMSF
TAX RATES	47%	30% 25%	0%	15% 0%
TAX PLANNING	✗	✓	✓	✓✓
ASSET PROTECTION	✗	✓*	✓*	✓✓

Also, if you are looking at the above diagram and seeing trusts at 0%, then that is a bit of a trick, because trusts don't pay tax ordinarily. They give it to other individuals or entities in the family group, and then they pay the tax on the share of income they received from the trust.

With superannuation, we are looking at a tax rate of 15% or 0% - and that 0% tax rate is legitimate.

The 15% tax rate applies when you are accumulating your balance throughout your lifetime, and when we refer to a member in this mode, we are saying that the member is in the accumulation phase.

Accumulting   **Drawing (Pension)**

15%   0%

The 0% tax is when you've met a condition of release and you are drawing a pension in line with pension requirements. Your earnings in your super fund relating to your pension portion are treated as tax-free.

There used to be no limit on this. So, even members with $10 million in super earning $1,000,000 a year in profit would pay no tax if they met the right conditions. But a couple of years ago, they brought in a maximum amount of your superannuation that can be tax-free, and the balance of your account would be taxed at 15%. This is still a very good outcome again, if we compare it to the individual tax rate or the company tax rates.

For anyone looking to find out more on these limits: they came into effect on 1 July 2017, and started with a cap of $1.6 million. It has now increased to a $1.7 million cap due to inflation as of 1 July 2021, and we expect to see more adjustments to this over the years.

The next thing I want to do is illustrate the power of that tax-free pension tax rate.

Let's say that you and your spouse purchased a commercial property for $1 million when you were 50 years old. Let's say that 15 years later, you are now 65, and the property is now worth $2 million. If you owned that in your SMSF, you could sell that asset and, assuming you meet pension requirements and limits, you could literally make a $1,000,000 capital gain on that property and pay $0 in tax.

Similarly, there are ways to own businesses in your SMSF and have the profits be distributed to your SMSF. You could literally have a share of profit of $1,000,000 go into an SMSF tax-free.

Again, this requires the right pension requirements, observation of limits, and an ownership structure that does not breach any superannuation or tax rules. It's fantastic and something that I believe business owners should consider especially in their late 40s, 50s and 60s to maximise the benefits of this low or no tax environment.

To illustrate the point around the low tax environment, in the table above, I've given three different examples of a starting investment at $100,000. Each year, $55,000 is added to each of these scenarios, reduced by the relevant tax rate for a contribution. The starting balance in each

Option		Option 1	Option 2	Option 3
Tax rate		30%	15%	0%
How		Bucket company	Accumulation	Pension
Starting balance		$100,000	$100,000	$100,000
Finanical year				
	2022	$144,100	$153,550	$154,750
	2023	$296,270	$317,541	$321,880
	2024	$456,961	$492,684	$502,380
	2025	$626,650	$679,737	$697,321
	2026	$805,843	$879,509	$907,856
	2027	$995,070	$1,092,865	$1,135,235
	2028	$1,194,894	$1,320,730	$1,380,804
	2029	$1,405,908	$1,564,090	$1,646,018
	2030	$1,628,739	$1,823,998	$1,932,450
	2031	$1,864,048	$2,101,580	$2,241,796
Net benefit vs bucket company			$237,532	$377,747

year plus the annual contribution earns an investment return of 8% less tax. I picked $55,000, as it's the total annual concessional contribution limit of $27,500 each, for two people.

The bucket company is our base scenario entity with a 30% tax rate. You can see after 10 years even the accumulation mode or a 15% tax rate has a difference in investment outcome of $237,532 due to the reduced tax rate. If we take it a step further, we can see that the pension fund with a 0% tax rate show an even bigger difference long term of $377,747 compared with the bucket company.

In summary, there are some fantastic tax outcomes when it comes to SMSFs.

Investment Strategy

The next thing we need to have a look at is the super fund's investment strategy.

It is a requirement of the fund to have a documented investment strategy – and it needs to be kept up to date. If this isn't the case, then you run the risk of a reported breach of the Superannuation Act.

While this becomes something else for the trustees of a SMSF to do, I feel it is a benefit. Why? Because it forces the trustees of the fund to have a very organised approach to the way that they care for the money they have been entrusted to invest.

The things that investment strategy should consider are:

- The type investments the super fund will invest in

- The potential risks of the investments

- The level of diversification of investments

- The benchmark for different classes of investment assets (this is a benchmark for how much of the funds total assets will be made up by each asset class)

- The intended return on investments

- Any considerations with borrowings for the fund

- Insurance for the members of the fund (they don't need to take out insurance, but it needs to be considered for everyone)

- Liquidity and cash flow requirements (for paying debt or paying out pensions)

An investment strategy is not just *set and forget*. It should be reviewed each year and updated, if required. Also, a few notes on the choice of investments the fund can make:

- Make sure they are permitted under the SMSF's deed

- That they are not prohibited investments by the Superannuation Act

- That they comply with the 'sole purpose test'

The sole purpose test means that your fund needs to be maintained for the sole purpose of providing retirement benefits to your members, or death benefits to their dependents, if a member dies before retirement.

Examples of breaches of the sole purpose test might be:

- Investing in a holiday house but you stay in it in between hosting paying guests

- Lending money to a member of the fund in their own name

- Buying a residential property and having a related party or family member living in it

- Buying personal use assets or collectables displayed by or leased to a related party

This is not a complete list of every example of a breach of the sole purpose test, but it provides a guide to the type of thing you can't do with your funds money or investments.

Leverage

The next benefit to run through is the ability for an SMSF to borrow money and leverage their own cash position.

LRBA - Limited Recourse Borrowing Arrangement

SMSF cannot borrow to buy property directly

Bare Trust sits in the middle as a "shadow" purchasing entity
- can be borrowed from a bank
- can be you own cash (bucket company)

An SMSF cannot borrow money directly in its own right, but it uses a bare trust to sit in between the SMSF and the asset it is purchasing. We call these special requirements for lending to SMSF's 'limited recourse borrowing arrangements' or LRBA's. Cash can be borrowed from a bank, which is the most common, but money can also be borrowed from your own entities (such as a bucket company) to purchase an asset.

In terms of the broad lending rules, one of the things that we usually do is show our clients the difference between what the normal environment looks like when lending outside super versus inside super.

OUTSIDE SUPER	VS	INSIDE SUPER (SMSF)
• Slightly less complex lending • Higher tax outcome • Business/personal income to service. Can adjust for existing rent if you will owner occupy • Can use other security for deposit	**BOTH** • Can owner occupy • Can see LVR's go to 80%	• "LRBA" • Super contributions and rental income to service • Tax 15% or 0$ • Very few lenders (Still good) • Typically higher rate • Lender can require advice (legal and financial planning) • Needs cash deposit • Cannot borrow for constructions costs unless off plan

Some of the pros and cons can be seen in the table above, but one of the great things is that usually, your borrowing capacity in your SMSF doesn't have to rely on any borrowing capacity outside of super.

In terms of the deposit required, there are some lenders who will lend 80% of your property value depending on the postcode and the asset type that you're buying. But, it is common for most lenders in the space to lend at least 70% of most assets.

That means that you will need to have between a 20 to 30% deposit plus stamp duty, and often have a little bit of cash leftover in your fund after settlement to pay the bills and other expenses of the fund. Some lenders want to see about 10% of your property value in liquid cash after settlement.

At the end of the day, the details here depend on the property that you are looking to purchase and the lenders you are working with. My recommendation is to speak to a mortgage broker who has experience in SMSF lending, and let them do the running around to match you to the best lender for what you're looking to do.

The other thing to keep in mind is that you can only borrow for one single asset. What this means is you can't purchase something like a house and land package where there are two separate contracts, and you are funding the land purchase and the construction costs separately.

You can purchase an off-the-plan property from a developer where there is a single contract, though. You even need to watch out for properties that have two titles such as commercial properties across two titles. There are sometimes ways around this where you take out two loans, but this can prove a bit tricky when the goal is to meet the superannuation rules but also to keep in line with what the lender requires.

Property is the most common asset that is purchased using lending in super. You can also borrow money to purchase other assets such as a single set of shares. Even though you are buying more than one share, if it's a single ASX listed share and you're buying a parcel of them, the rules are written so that this is considered a single acquirable asset.

So, you could buy, as an example, 100 BHP shares as a parcel and have a loan on that. But if you were to take a loan out to purchase 50 BHP shares and 50 Rio Tinto shares under the same loan agreement, then that will not work for the single acquirable asset rule.

The other thing just before we wrap up the leverage section is to mention that if you are borrowing money from your own entity like a bucket company, then the loan has to be on commercial terms. Please be careful with this and seek advice if this is what you are planning to do.

Insurance

One of the things that you should consider with your SMSF is insurance.

This is a requirement for your investment strategy of the fund, where you need to consider insurance for each member. That doesn't necessarily mean that every member will need insurance, but rather it has at least been considered and there is a documented decision as to why a member has or has not taken up insurance.

Some of the benefits of taking out insurance in an SMSF are:

- Certain insurances, such as life insurance and TPD, are tax-deductible to the fund (Let's compare that to my life insurance policy held outside of super where there is no tax deduction available personally)

- Payments for the cost of the insurance are made from the SMSF member's balance rather than the member themselves, which can help personal cash flow

- In an SMSF, you can customise the policy and the provider to the member, whereas in certain industry funds there are usually only group policies available

There are a couple of negatives to know for insurance held in super:

- The premium payments reduce your balance, which can have a compounding negative effect, especially if you are not contributing at least as much as the insurance premium each year

- The insurance payment is paid to the fund rather than the member directly. This means the member has to go through the process of getting it out of the fund by meeting the conditions of release. There may be instances where the insurance payment is triggered to the fund, but the member cannot legally withdraw that insurance pay-out due to not meeting a condition of release.

Incapacity Planning

You should also consider incapacity, if you are a member of a SMSF.

This is where you are still alive but you don't have the capacity to make financial decisions.

An enduring power of attorney is a tool where, on incapacity, you can defer your decision-making to a nominated person or a set of people. You must arrange this in advance though, as you cannot execute an enduring power of attorney if you have already lost capacity.

An SMSF requires all members to be either trustees or directors of the fund. You are able to be a member and nominate someone to be a director on your behalf through an enduring power of attorney. The power of attorney must be set up correctly, but the SMSF deed also needs to be reviewed to make sure this is an allowable setup.

Estate Planning

In the previous step, we spoke about estate planning, so I won't cover this in detail here.

I just want to cover some key points relating to superannuation and SMSF's specifically:

- Your superannuation proceeds after you pass away are dealt with by a binding death benefit nomination, ideally to give you the certainty of where your balance will go

- Failing that, the trustee of the fund will decide what happens with your balance, if you have no nomination in place

- Keep in mind that even if you've got a small superannuation balance, but you hold a life insurance policy in super, it may turn out to be a significant asset of your estate, therefore this needs care and planning

- Your super balance can be paid to your estate and dealt with under your Will, or it could also be paid to a person specifically. This skips your Will and can remove the ability for that super balance to be contested

- If your super balance is paid to a non-dependent, then you can pay 17% tax on the taxable component of your balance

Some Cool Things You Can Do With Your SMSF

Buy commercial or residential property

Residential   **Commercial**

An SMSF can be used to purchase a commercial or residential property.

When it comes to residential property, a member or a related person of a member cannot live in (owner occupy) that property. But, it's still a fantastic way to grow your superannuation balance by investing in high-quality residential property.

You can also borrow money from banks, as I've mentioned earlier in this section. This can mean that if you've got a few hundred thousand dollars in super, you may be able to buy a fairly significant property with help from lenders.

In terms of commercial property though, a member's business or even a related party's business *can* rent a commercial property that's owned in that person's SMSF. So, the difference is that the business can owner occupy the property, if it is a commercial property. This means that you can use your SMSF in a way that may benefit your business by securing a commercial property which helps both the long-term stability and growth of your business.

You are essentially both the tenant and the landlord, where your business is the tenant and you are the landlord through your own SMSF. While that may be the case, there are requirements for you to make sure that the rent is market rate, and this should be confirmed or documented where the auditor of your fund also checks this.

Become your own bank

Another thing you can do with your SMSF is to lend to other people or entities.

There are restrictions on lending money to members themselves. But, if you have a related party business, there is a way to lend up to 5% of the value of the total assets in the SMSF to that related party business. This is seen as an in-house asset and is heavily scrutinised by the auditor and reportable to the ATO in the tax return. As long as it's on market-rate terms and it does not exceed 5% of the total assets of the fund, there are not too many things that can unwind this.

A bit of a trap here is this. Say that you've got $1,000,000 in your SMSF in value, most of which is invested in the stock market. If you were to lend $50,000 to a related party business, this would be exactly 5% of your total fund balance. If in the next month, the share market lost 20% of its value, your $50,000 loan would now be worth 6.25% of the total value of the fund, therefore breaching the in-house asset rules.

Because of this, we often caution people who are looking to explore this option with the example above, and make sure they are constantly monitoring what is happening with the total value of the fund if they are close to lending the 5% maximum.

The other alternative is that you can lend money to a non-related party and this is not seen as an in-house asset.

An example of how people have used this in the past is by lending a friend money to start their business or fund growth in their business. As with most things with SMSFs, care needs to be taken to make sure everything is done carefully and at market rate value.

The interest rate relative to what the loan is for, relative to the security taken, the term provided, and the repayment terms are all very important and must be right. This is extremely high risk, especially if there is limited security taken for the loan. Risk and diversification need to be considered in the investment strategy for the fund.

In summary, I wouldn't ever recommend people set up an SMSF to loan money out (nor am I able to advise from a financial planning perspective on what an SMSF should invest in) – but an SMSF *can* do these things, assuming that the right documentation is put in place.

Invest in private companies or trusts

Another thing that an SMSF can invest in is private companies, or private unit trusts.

There are some restrictions around this, where the SMSF or its related parties cannot have control through an ownership share of more than 50%, or even perceived control through influence on other parties, nor a tie-breaker ability (in the case of shareholders where sharedholders disagree).

There must be a genuine inability to control the entity, but even an 'ownership share' of 50% is possible. This being the case, if you have two or more business partners, you can technically set up companies or trusts with your super funds providing the start-up capital, and then run a business that is owned by super.

Another example of this is you can start up an investment entity where you have multiple families investing in a big project or investment, such as property development, a large property purchase, or an investment fund.

Again, anything like this needs to be done with care and should always be done with the right advice.

Develop property

Another thing that we see very commonly done with SMSF's is where a family group develops property. Now, the cool thing about this is that there are many ways to structure a property development that incorporate your super balance.

A few years ago, I met a group of four potential business partners. They were looking to do a property development using money that each one had saved plus equity in their houses. The development size they were thinking about was around the $2 to $4 million mark.

They all had some form of experience in developments larger than that $2-4M range through their current and previous employment history, but they thought that they were limited in development size based solely on their available equity in savings.

One of those four people was a client of Inspire. The client organised a property development structuring session including all four of them, using us as advisers. By the end of that session, we were able to talk through how they could use their combined super balances to significantly increase their development equity position. In turn, this would allow them to access more funding and be able to do a larger development.

After that session, they have been hunting for larger developments, given the increased scope, and have recently begun the process on a $10 million development. This is much more than they thought they could access previously, all thanks to the power of using their super balance to assist.

We've also seen situations where two unrelated family groups come together to fund a small development through super, and even engage a related-party builder to complete the construction, if there are houses to be built.

There are about half a dozen ways that we have structured this type of thing in the past where everaging superannuation opens up more options for either development size or cash flow. We have also created options around where the bulk of the profit goes, whether that is inside or outside of super.

Of course, all of these options are extremely complex, and I'm proud to say that our team have a bit of a speciality (and a genuine interest) in getting the most out of the situation for the maximum benefit of the client. So, if you do want to talk more about this, we have options for running property development structuring sessions like this that incorporate super. Please reach out for a strategy call if this is something you are keen on exploring.

SMSF Success Stories

SMSF Success Story 1: The Vet from the Bush

The first case study I'd like to chat through is what I call the Vet from the bush.

He came to us having purchased a vet practice from another vet, who was exiting the industry, a few years beforehand. In the purchase, he also purchased the building and land that the previous vet had practised from.

Unfortunately, the business and the land were both purchased in his own name as a sole trader. For reasons which I'll go deep into in my book *It's All Sorted*, this is not ideal, for both tax and asset protection reasons.

The property was worth around $300,000 with a soon-expiring temporary loan from the bank for $150,000. The equity position, therefore, was $150,000. One option that we calculated the numbers on for him, was to move the ownership of the property into his SMSF.

This would require paying a small amount of stamp duty on the transfer. Also, because he didn't have the full $300,000 in his super fund, his super fund would need a loan of the difference between his super balance and the total purchase price of $300,000, plus stamp duty.

He had around $170,000 in super and, to square things off, the goal was to pay the deposit of $150,000 plus stamp duty and have a few thousand to spare in his fund after the transaction. This meant that he needed a loan value of around $150,000 lent to his super fund.

Now, we could have loaned that money from a bank. We ran the numbers and he decided to vendor finance the $150,000, which meant lending the money from his own company into his SMSF to purchase the property *from* him as a sole trader.

So he sold the property to his SMSF and the SMSF paid him $150,000 upfront, which he used to clear the bank loan. Then he is essentially owed the balance of $150,000 from his SMSF, which he can get paid back as the SMSF accrues more money through the rental income or the additional contributions it receives.

Now his business can pay say $20,000 of rent into the SMSF. Then compling with his loan agreement, he could literally transfer that $20,000 back to his company account as a repayment of his vendor finance loan.

Similarly, he could use his concessional contributions cap (which is $27,500 at the time of writing this book), transfer this money into his SMSF as a contribution, and use some or all of that amount to repay the vendor finance agreement. (Note that some of this needs to be set aside for contributions tax.)

He can continue to do these loops of paying money into the fund and back out through the vendor finance agreement, until the vendor finance agreement has been completely paid out.

This sort of situation can provide opportunities to put money into the SMSF as tax-deductible contributions or rent, and then receive the cash straight back, which can be a significant help for cash flow, either personally or in the business.

SMSF Success Story 2: $300,000 Tax-Free Gain

Another scenario I want to share was from several years ago.

I worked with a client who owned a commercial property worth around $1,000,000 outside of super. This case study involved transferring the ownership of the property into super as well, which we needed to do at a market rate value.

The client had around $300,000 in super, so we needed to loan $700,000, which came from the bank. Before he moved it (while it was held outside of super), the property had a loan on it. This was paid out once the SMSF purchased the property from him.

Over the next 24 - 36 months, the property increased in value by around $300,000 to approximately $1.3 million.

The client had an opportunity to sell this property for this amount. When he did, he made a $300,000 capital gain while paying $0.00 in tax. The reason this happened is that the two members of the SMSF were drawing a tax-free pension from super.

Over these few years, the client's super balance effectively more than doubled, due to the gain and contributions that had been made throughout that time.

SMSF Success Story 3: IT Business From Melbourne

The third case study I want to share was from a client whose business grew rapidly through the global COVID-19 pandemic.

The business owner had an opportunity to buy a larger office space than the one they were renting. This was the right pathway for them, and it was also close to their home. The purchase price was around $300,000 and the space needed a small fit-out before they could run their business from that space. The client took a loan from the bank, as they only had a combined amount of around $120,000 in super, due to being a young family.

Now, in terms of the fit-out the office required, you cannot borrow under superannuation rules for construction or fit-out. The client's SMSF didn't have enough cash after the purchase to spend $50,000 on a fitout. So, what we did instead was organise for the client's business to prepay a year's worth of market-rate rent of around $25,000. Then,

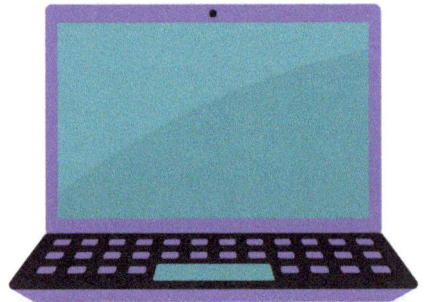

the client made superannuation contributions to make up the difference of $25,000 - what they needed for that fit out.

The client is now paying similar rent to what he was beforehand when renting from a third party, but it is a bigger space to allow for the growth of his business *and* he is paying rent into his own SMSF. This means he is therefore increasing his wealth at the same time.

SMSF Final Words

In summary, I believe that SMSF's are a fantastic way for business owners to grow their wealth and they provide far more flexibility than standard retail or industry super funds.

There is a lot of work that goes into the setup and running an administration and compliance of an SMSF, so I would never recommend that anyone sets one up or runs one without the help of advisers who specialise in the field.

Inspire also has additional webinar recordings and information available on our YouTube channel regarding SMSF's. All of our partners and managers at Inspire are well versed in the ins and outs of what we've covered in this step. If you would like our assistance, all you need to do is reach out for a strategy call and we can see if we can help you with what you're looking to achieve.

Part Summary

I hope you enjoyed learning about the structures involved in creating wealth for life, from insurances to estate planning and the 'ins and outs' of SMSF's.

You may have noticed that, so far, we haven't gone into detail yet about types of investments like shares or property. This is very intentional, because we want to make sure you are very clear on where you are aiming to go and that you have the right structures in place first, which has been the focus of the six steps up until now.

Moving forward, we're going to discuss investing. This will include general investment methodologies and theories all the way through a deep dive into property investment and rounding out with the final step by discussing how you can make the most out of debt.

Implementation Checklist

Step 4	
Have you considered the different types of insurance you would like?	☐
Have you reviewed your existing insurances or reached out to an adviser?	☐
Step 5	
Have you reviewed your estate planning and Will in the last two years?	☐
Have you completed the **1 Page Estate Plan?**	☐
Step 6	
Have you considered if an SMSF is a good option for you?	☐
Have you discussed any potential investments you are interested to make in an SMSF with an adviser?	☐

PART 3: Growth

n the next section, we are going to talk about making wise investment decisions to help grow your wealth.

Now, I've mentioned this earlier in the book, but I do want to remind you that I am not a licensed financial adviser, therefore I cannot make any financial product recommendations. What I will do though, is share broader wealth creation strategies and philosophies that I've learned over my lifetime from other mentors and authors. I will also share my own perspectives on investing.

We'll then cover some benefits of including property as part of your family's investment strategy. Then, we will wrap up with a discussion around leveraging debt, as it can be super powerful when it is used the right way.

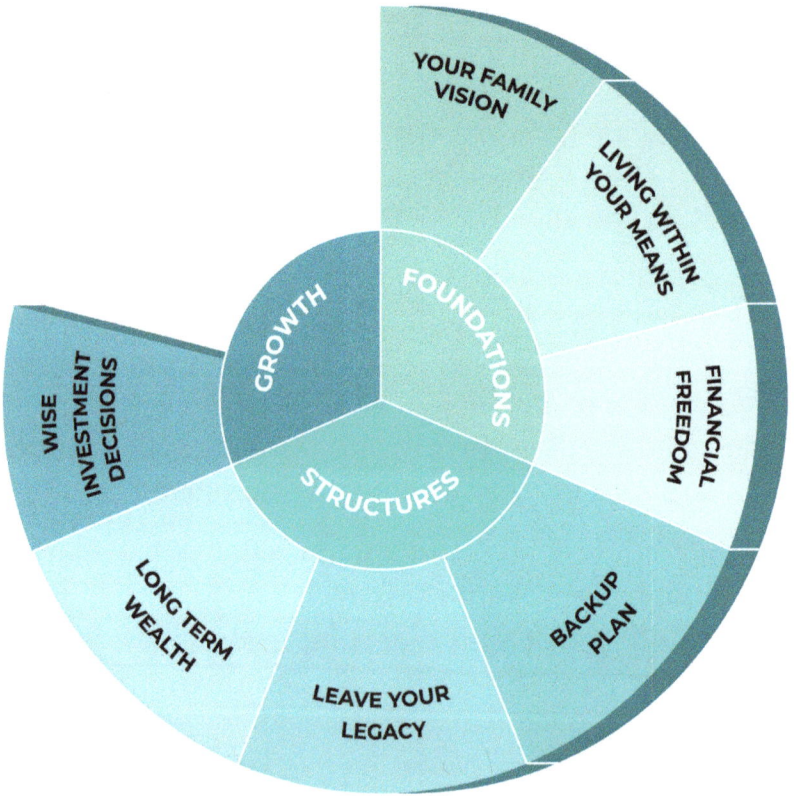

Center:
GROWTH · FOUNDATIONS · STRUCTURES

Outer segments:
YOUR FAMILY VISION
LIVING WITHIN YOUR MEANS
FINANCIAL FREEDOM
BACKUP PLAN
LEAVE YOUR LEGACY
LONG TERM WEALTH
WISE INVESTMENT DECISIONS

Step 7:
Wise Investment Decisions

"Compound interest is the eighth wonder of the world. He who understands it, earns it ... he who doesn't, pays it."

Albert Einstein

If I could have done things differently in my life, I would have started my investment journey earlier, and put effort into it with more consistency. There is a Chinese proverb that says that the best time to plant a tree was 20 years ago. The second-best time is *now*. The purpose of this step is to share the philosophies I have on investments and to encourage you to start putting money away and investing for your family.

Four Types of Investments

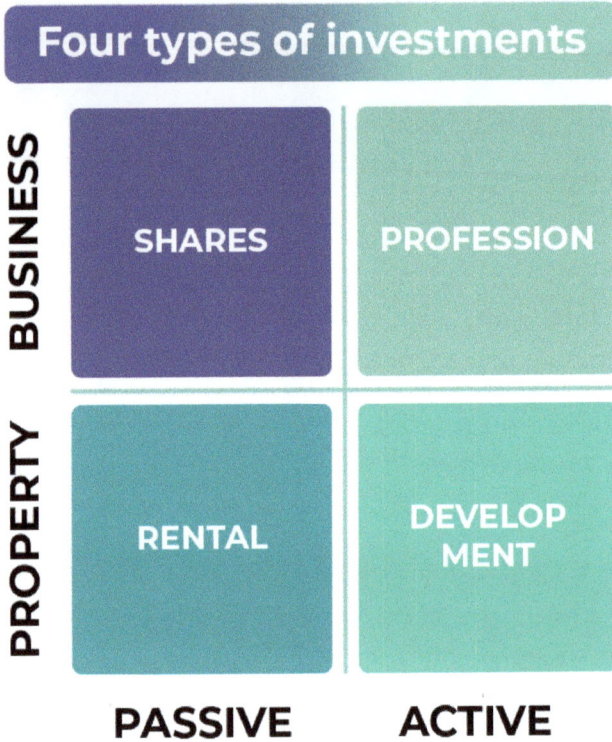

Four types of investments

	PASSIVE	ACTIVE
BUSINESS	SHARES	PROFESSION
PROPERTY	RENTAL	DEVELOPMENT

The first thing I want to share with regards to investing is a model that makes it easy for me to categorise where my efforts and money are going. My goal in sharing this is to simplify the world of investments.

In the model above, I have categorised everything into **four types of investments**.

You have property or business on the Y axis (the vertical one), and passive or active investments on the X axis (the horizontal one).

Now, I just want to clarify my definitions here: I don't believe that *any* investment is truly passive in the sense that you don't need any time energy or resources to invest in it. So, when I refer to the word passive, it is meant to mean that a lot less energy time and resources goes into managing the passive investments than for the active ones.

So, in the **passive investments** category, you've got **property** or **business**. Passive property investments are rental properties, such as a rental house or commercial property that you lease out to tenants, usually on a long-term basis.

In the **passive business** space, you've got investments into **shares**. I also include managed funds or ETF's or even unlisted funds in this box. Essentially, what you're doing is giving your money to another business so that they can invest on your behalf. You then receive a return from the profit it makes and the capital growth it experiences through owning a small percentage of it.

On the **active invsetments** side of the model, you've also got **property** and **business**. Active business means the profession or career or literal business that you run (for me, that is Inspire).

The reason why I want to show this box as an investment is that I feel like *all* business owners should treat their business like it should be returning a profit *and* growing in value. Just like you would expect a return of profit and capital growth if you're investing in any other box on this model, we need to expect that from the cash, energy, and time that we invest into our businesses. We shouldn't be running a business just to earn a wage or a salary on its own.

The last category is **active property investments**, which I refer to as property development. My perspective on property development is where you take an existing property asset (like land, or an existing house and land), and develop that into something that is worth more in value and that provides more for the community.

So, the developer who goes through that process, should be rewarded with profit on that development. Property development definitely comes with much greater risk, but also higher potential returns than passive property investments.

I do acknowledge that there are also other classes of investments such as currency, cryptocurrency, precious metals, collectables and so on, but what I want to do with this model is simply give you a high-level overview and framework in which to think about investments. This is helpful especially for those who aren't well versed in what investment types are available to them.

I also feel like some of these other investment classes I refer to require specialist knowledge in each of the fields. Therefore, I do see any investment in these classes as active investing, not passive.

My own personal perspective is to make sure I've got investments in the different categories I have drawn in the model above. This is so that all my eggs are not in the one basket. I make sure that I've got multiple income streams as well as having multiple ways to achieve capital growth.

What I've Seen Work With Investing

The Power of Compound Returns

Example of Compounding of Savings at 8 Percent

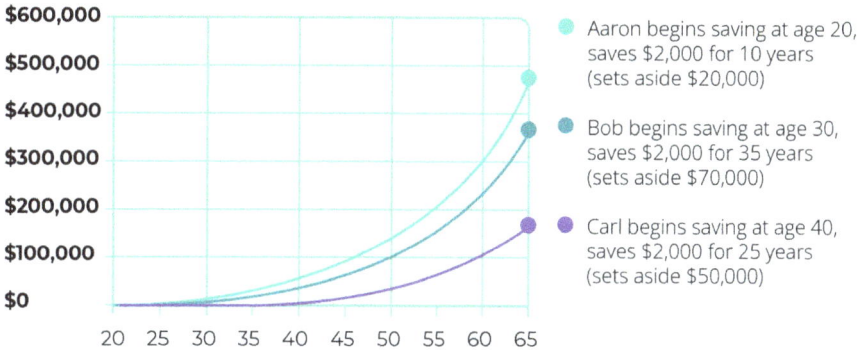

Aaron begins saving at age 20, saves $2,000 for 10 years (sets aside $20,000)

Bob begins saving at age 30, saves $2,000 for 35 years (sets aside $70,000)

Carl begins saving at age 40, saves $2,000 for 25 years (sets aside $50,000)

The power of compound returns is very valuable to you as an investor.

The graph above provides three examples that show what compounding savings can produce over a person's lifetime.

All of the scenarios above show what the result will be if the investment earns a compounding return of 8% a year. That means if there was a $10,000 investment, an 8% return on this would earn $800 in the first year, taking the investment to a value of $10,800. In year two, the 8% return on this would be $864, taking the total investment to $11,664, and so on (the returns grow on the increased amount each year).

The green line in the graph is Aaron. Aaron started saving when he was 20 years old and he invests $2,000 per year for ten years. So, he has only invested a total of $20,000 over ten years. By the time he is 65 years old, that total amount invested of $20,000 will be worth around $500,000.

Now, let's have a look at the blue line, Bob. Bob start saving 10 years later than Aaron did when he was age 30. He saves the same amount of $2,000 a year for 35 years, through to the age of 65. When he's 65, even though he invested $70,000 in total, because he started later than Aaron did, he only ends up with just shy of $400,000.

To further exacerbate the scenario of waiting another few years later to start investing, let's have a look at the yellow line, Carl. Carl begins investing at age 40 where he saves $2,000 a year for 25 years or setting aside $50,000 in total.

By age 65, his amount is worth around $180,000 – around about half of what Bob ended up with at the end of the day. This clearly shows how even if you save more over your lifetime but you start saving later, it can have a huge impact on your overall wealth later down the line.

The best time to start investing was when you first started earning an income. But, if you haven't been doing it consistently, then the second-best time to start investing, if you haven't already, is right now. Even if you don't know exactly what you want to invest in just yet, setting aside the money to invest is the first step to making it grow.

Money Makes Money

One of the significant things I have noticed as I've grown my own personal wealth is that *'money makes money'*. It seems to be a magnet to attract more money or returns to your initial investment.

I heard a quote from Charlie Munger, a billionaire investor and philanthropist:

"The first $100,000 is a bitch, but you gotta do it. I don't care what you have to do. If it means walking everywhere and not eating anything that wasn't purchased with a coupon, find a way to get your hands on $100,000. After that, you can ease off the gas a little bit."

While I found this quote amusing, I also reflected on my own journey and found that to be 100% true. Accumulating the first $100,000 of liquid investments took over a decade of working, but the speed at which that $100,000 turned into $200,000 and so on, has been exponentially faster.

Out of curiosity, I did a bit of research into why this is the case. There are potentially a few different reasons for it, depending on your individual circumstances:

- If you've got money already set aside, you might be more likely to take higher risks than someone who is still accumulating the first $100,000. With higher risks, generally, come higher rewards.

- The power of compound returns continues to speed up the rate at which you build up your investments.

- You are able to instantly take advantage of opportunities that come up if you have cash set aside, such as undervalued real estate, or a great business opportunity that will return money to you quickly.

- As time passes, the amount you can contribute to your investments might increase, through increased salary or business profits.

- You have embedded habits that have allowed you to accrue the $100,000 which makes it easier to do it again and again.

So, if you haven't reached your first $100,000 in investments just yet, then I recommend that you make this your first goal. Do whatever it takes to get there,as after this point, it will become easier to continue to grow your investments and create the wealth you want for yourself and your family.

Diversification

Another sensible concept is diversification.

This is taught to us when we were kids when we heard the saying, "Don't put all your eggs in one basket." When it comes to investing, the idea of diversification is that if you bet on the wrong horse (so to speak), then you don't want to be in a position where you have lost all of your investment capital. But if you spread your bets out, to let's say three horses instead of one, and one of them loses but the other two come second and third, then you have lost a lot less money than the person who bet all their money on the wrong horse.

That is why, I shared the model with the four different classes of investments when I started this step: **business** versus **property** and **active** versus **passive**. While some of those quadrants are weighted more heavily than others in my own family's investment strategy, I do keep an eye on the quadrants that I have a lower allocation to. This is to make sure that I have some focus on holding that diversification.

Even if you only primarily want to invest in one asset class, it is not wise to have all of your investments inside one listed share or, if you're in property investments, to not purchase all of your property in the same postcode. What if your share in particular tanked, or most of the suburb that you were invested in, flooded in a freak flood (like we've seen in recent years)?

Diversification is not a complicated concept to grasp. The simple idea is to make sure that your investments are diversified so that you don't have a significant risk in one asset class or subcategory within an asset class.

Dollar Cost Averaging

Another concept of investing is one that aligns with the power of the compound returns strategy above, the idea of **dollar cost averaging**.

The practice of dollar cost averaging is where, if you have a large sum to invest in an investment – let's say the share market – then you don't just invest that whole sum at once. Instead, you invest it consistently over weeks or months, maybe even years. Now, why would we want to do this? It is to ride out any short-term gains or losses that the share market provides, that may affect your initial investment capital.

For instance, if you had $10,000 to invest, and you invest it all on a Monday, and the share market tanked on Tuesday, down by 20% and it stayed at that level for the rest of the week, then you are instantly down 20%, to a value of $8,000.

But, if you were to invest 1/5th of that $10,000 equally over the days of that week between Monday, Tuesday, Wednesday, Thursday and Friday, then the amount that you invested on Monday would have also dropped by 20%. But Monday's investment was only $2,000 which is now worth $1,600.

For the remaining days, you also invested $2,000 per day. This means that your total investment at the end of this week would be worth $9,600. While you've still lost some money, this means you end up with 20% more in investment value compared with the first scenario.

So, dollar cost averaging is a way of protecting your initial investment capital.

It is also a great way to make ongoing investments into your portfolio. Instead of say dumping $50,000 into a share portfolio once a year, splitting this up into monthly or weekly investments would be less risky, for the same reason we just discovered above.

What Doesn't Work When It Comes To Investing

As well as sharing the concepts and philosophies on what I've seen work really well when it comes to investing, I do want to share some things that I have seen that did not go well. These lessons are from either my own investing or from clients I've worked with.

Not taking action

The first one is not taking action.

I'm not referring to having the inability to invest due to a lack of money. This is more so where you have the ability to invest, but you keep thinking about reasons why it won't work, such as:

- It's too risky.

- It's not the right time.

- I'm not sure I could deal with the stress.

- Is this the right opportunity, or is there another one coming?

All of those things are healthy questions or things to consider. But, if you're in a cycle of constantly *not* taking action on any opportunity that comes to you, then it is likely that you are also passing up any reward that you might get from investments.

For instance, I've seen people hesitate to buy property and then, over the coming years, they've seen other people make a killing because real estate boomed. I've also seen people who knew about cryptocurrency for ten years when Bitcoin was worth $0.10 or even $10. While, yes, this is an extremely risky investment, they weren't even keen to chuck a few hundred bucks on in the early days (this was me, too!!!).

What I am saying here is that even if there are valid reasons for you not yet having invested, I would encourage you to get help from a professional adviser to help overcome those barriers, as your money is going to go backwards if it is left sitting in a bank account being eaten away by inflation.

Timing the market

This one is also related to not taking action, except the idea is that you are sitting out on investing because you're waiting to time the market 'right'.

Unfortunately, what most people do here is that they make emotional decisions. This means that they buy when the market has gone up (or is still going up), but waiting until the market starts rising before you invest money will result in you missing the initial uplift in value while you wait.

The other thing that happens a lot – and I saw this especially in the 2008 GFC – is that when the market goes down, people sell, thinking that the market is going to completely crash. So, in the example of the GFC, they might have taken a 30, 40 or 50% hit, and sold out. Then, the market picked up over the coming months and years, rising to *above* where it was in the first place. This means that if you sold out when the market dropped, you experienced a massive loss and missed the chance to ride the wave back up again.

While people have made (and do still make) money out of timing the market, it is an extremely dangerous place to play for new or inexperienced investors, where emotions may take control at the wrong moment. I've even seen experienced investors make this mistake in recent years.

Picking winners

The other thing I've seen go wrong quite often with investing is when a person tries to consistently pick winners for their investments.

Whether it is cryptocurrency coins or shares, or any other asset class, what usually happens is that people get excited over the potential of some things that they think are going to grow very fast in value. Sometimes this does happen, which is great, but there is a lot of time where it is just pure speculation. In these cases, nothing happens, or that investment actually *loses* value.

There is even research that proves that the vast majority of stockbrokers who are essentially paid to pick winners, cannot outperform the market average compound returns of the stock market (i.e., just dollar cost averaging and continual investing over a sustained amount of time).

So, unless you have inside information as to why some investment is about to go crazy (which is illegal in most countries), it's best to steer clear of this and consider any investment you make in this way a gamble.

Expecting returns too early

This graphic stands out to me when I think about how people sometimes expect returns from their investments too early. The truth is that there are limited ways to get rich quick, and if that's what you're looking for, then you'll have a very low chance of making it happen.

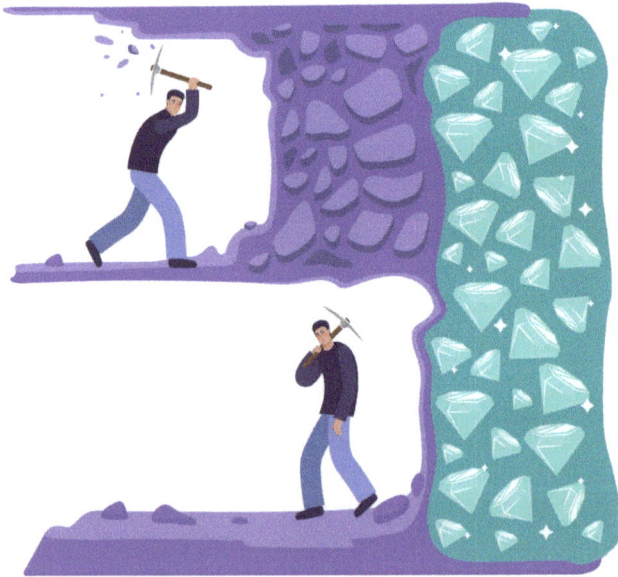

Most sustainable financial wealth is built over years or decades, not weeks or months. One of the things I've personally done in the past is to sell out of an investment right before it went through the roof, because I wasn't patient enough to wait for it to mature. So, if you're getting a bit down because you're not making the returns that you wanted to, soon enough, then encourage yourself to keep putting your head down. Trust the process and, if you're doing the right things, it will happen.

Conclusion

I hope that these general investing principles and philosophies have helped you. In terms of taking action on this information, you can take it from here.

Personally, this means first taking stock of where your current investments are. Then, you can work out how much per month (or per year) you would like to contribute to more investments. A very easy way of doing this is to compare what you earn to the living expenses of your household. The difference ideally is used to either pay down debt or invest. (We covered these numbers in *Step 2: Living Within Your Means*)

Once you've calculated the monthly or yearly amount you would like to invest, the next step is to work out which asset classes you'd like to invest it into. If you can do this through regular investments, such as weekly or monthly contributions, this will get you great outcomes, as we discussed in the dollar cost averaging section.

If you're not keen to do this solo, and you need help with investing, please reach out to us. It is not so much that we can directly help you, but we can refer you to a financial planner that we have worked with for over a decade who has produced some great outcomes for our clients.

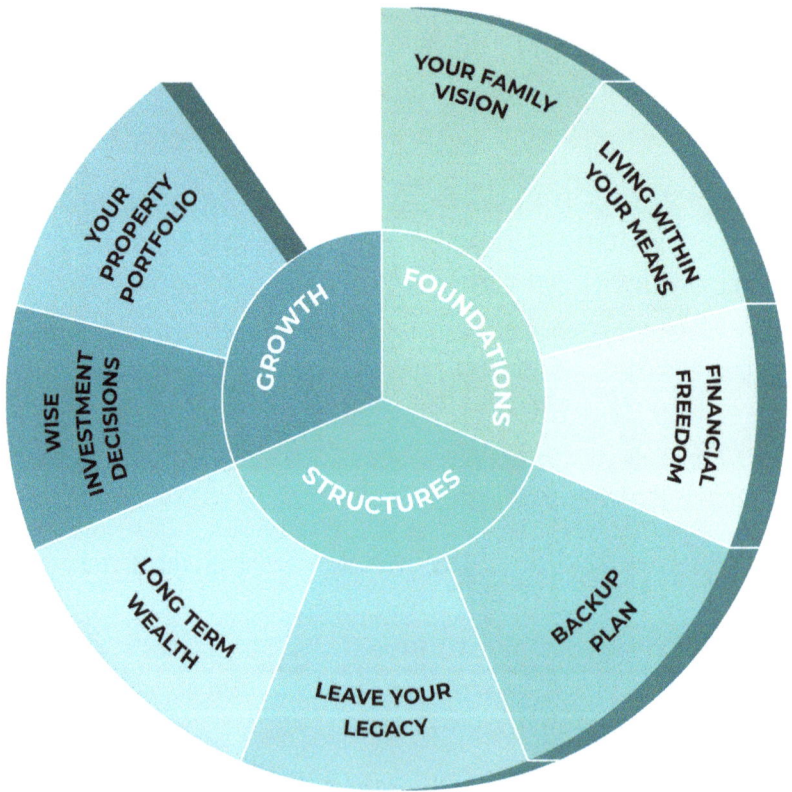

Step 8:
Your Property Portfolio

"Ninety percent of all millionaires become so through owning real estate. More money has been made in real estate than in all industrial investments combined."

Andrew Carnegie

Australians love investing in bricks and mortar, and there are great reasons to do it. If we look at our wealthiest clients, they all have property incorporated into their investment strategy. In fact, property is often a key component in what has led them to be in a wealthy position in the first place. I have heard the saying, "Success leaves clues," and I am taking the hint with this one, having incorporated property into my own wealth strategy.

Advantages Of Having Property In Your Portfolio

Some advantages of including property in your investment strategy include:

- **You get access to tax benefits, such as:**

  o Being able to claim depreciation. This is not a cash outlay each year, but you are claiming a small portion of the construction cost of the property each year.

  o Negative gearing. It is not that we necessarily want investment properties to cost us money each month, but some properties are negatively geared, which means they are creating a tax loss. It is possible to have a cash flow positive property where it is negatively geared at the same time, because of the depreciation tax deduction. If it makes a tax loss, then you can offset this against other income. Keep in mind that it is important which name that the property is purchased under, whether it's in a personal name or under a trust, will impact how this negative gearing benefit works.

  o The capital gains *main residence exemption* provides for tax-free gains on your own home, if you make a gain between when you buy it and when you sell it. For instance, if you were to buy your own home for $1,000,000 and sell it five years later for $2,000,000, and you have met the right conditions, then you will pay no tax on that $1,000,000 gain.

  o An often-unknown additional benefit to the main residence exemption is the six-year rule. This means that if you purchase a property to be your main residence and you live in it, if you were to move out of that property, then you have up to six years to sell that property where you can elect for the sale to be exempt for capital gains tax purposes.

There are a couple of things to keep in mind here. One of them is that you can't claim the capital gains tax exemption on more than one property at the same time. So, if you were to move out of your first property and purchase the second one to live in straight away, then you sell the first one just before the six-year mark, then you cannot claim the exemption on that same six-year period when you were to go on and sell the second property.

It's a bit complicated so make sure you check with an accountant before you rely on this one. It can be extremely useful if you were to own a main residence and move out of it for travel, or if you were to rent somewhere else for a few years and you still wanted to treat your initial property as capital gains tax-free once you sell it.

- Another benefit of property is that banks will easily lend money to purchase it, where you can leverage the bank's money and you end up getting a better return on yours (assuming it's a well performing property).

- You can touch and feel property. Some people prefer property just because of the fact that you can actually go and touch and feel it, as well as keep an eye on your investment. If you compare that to shares or money in the bank or cryptocurrency, they don't have that same physical appeal.

- It is often less exposed to stock market volatility. We can see this is evident even in the recent few years when the COVID-19 pandemic hit. The share market lost a huge percentage of value in the first month or two following the initial lockdowns. The real estate market in most capital cities in Australia stayed flat during that time, and then picked up massively towards the end of 2020 and onwards. If we have a look at that initial reaction that the stock market had, we did not see the same thing happen with real estate.

- With the right spending and debt setup, the property you own can help pay down your own home loan (more on this in the next step).

- You can live in a property if you ever wanted to or needed to. This is a nice but maybe often unused benefit for most investors, where they could live in their investment property if they ever had to, for whatever reason

What I Look For In My Own Property Strategy

Property forms most of our family's wealth outside of superannuation. Over the past few years, our family has bought and sold multiple properties. It was not that we planned it this way or knew that a boom was coming, but rather that we made the right decisions at the right time, in terms of getting into the market *before* it picked up.

Here are the key points I look at for my own property strategy:

- **Cash flow positive property.** Ideally the property is cash flow positive before any tax benefits. This is achievable, although it can be difficult if you are highly leveraged on the property. For instance, if you've borrowed more than 100% of the value of the property through a debt recycling strategy (more on that in *Step 9*), then it is tough because of the repayments required on a high level of debt.

- **Committed government spending.** I picked this up off a seasoned property investor. This is where they looked for areas where there was committed government spending to the area. These things signal from the government that there is a high proportion of the population moving to these areas, and that they need to increase their spending in those areas. If that is the case, then you can bet that there is money moving into that suburb or area as well. Here are some examples of what I mean by government spending:

  o Main roads/highways

  o New schools

  o New local amenities, like parks and stadiums

  o New transport investments, like trams or rail or bus hubs

- **Banks will easily lend on it.** The reason why this is important to me is more to do with the security of my own exit strategy, but also similar properties in the area will benefit from this, too.

What I mean when I say that banks will easily lend, is that banks have different policies on how much of a property's value they will lend depending on a number of different factors, such as the postcode it is in, and the size of it (too big or too small). What they are assessing is the risk, but also their ability to sell the property if you can't pay the loan, as well as how easily they will sell it to someone else.

For instance, there are some markets, such as Mount Isa in Queensland, which have experienced boom and bust over the past couple of decades with mining. Banks will not usually lend much more than 50 or 60% of the property's value when you purchase it. Let's we compare this to an inner-city suburb in Brisbane. As long as it's not a tiny studio apartment or student accommodation, on most houses, the banks will lend up to 90 or even 95% of the total value of them. This means that more people can purchase this property from you as they need a smaller percentage of the property value to purchase it using the banks' money. (i.e., they need a 5–20% deposit, rather than 50%)

- **High depreciation.** I look for properties that will give me high depreciation. This reduces the tax burden from investment income, while also increasing the cash flow we can earn on the property.

There are two types of depreciation you can claim. The first is a portion of the construction costs of the property over a 40-year straight-line method. The second one is claiming furniture and fittings, where the rate you can claim depends on the effective life of the asset. The depreciation rules were changed in 2017, where the second depreciation claim of furniture and fittings is only claimable if you purchase a brand-new property or build a new dwelling, like a house and land package.

If someone has lived in the property before you use it as an investment property, then you can only claim a percentage of the construction costs. This means that new property brings higher depreciation, and my focus has always been on finding a high-quality new property for this reason. Maintenance is generally very low on the brand new property, too, as most things are covered by the builder's warranties in the first few years.

- **I would live in it if I ever had to.** Each time we've purchased a property, I've considered the question "Would I choose to live here?". It's not that we ever have lived in one of our investment properties, but we do look for quality properties that provide a comfortable living space and conveniences that owner-occupiers might look for. This also helps when we want to sell a property and we can sell it to a potential owner-occupier who can emotionally buy into a property, rather than just an investor who will likely only look at the numbers. The other thing it provides is tenant appeal. This is where you will attract a higher quality tenant who may pay more because they are looking for this comfortable and convenient property to rent.

Running The Numbers On An Investment Property

It may help you if I run through the numbers that I look at when weighing up whether or not to invest in a property. This simple approach helps me to calculate what cash is required to purchase the property, but also what the expected return is on it. I've got a helpful spreadsheet I use for this, but the key data is below for you. I'll use an example of an apartment that we purchased in Windsor, Brisbane.

How much did we need to purchase it?

Property Value	$717,500
Deposit required %	10% (as banks lent us 90% without LMI)
Deposit required - $	$71,750
Stamp duty	$27,632
Conveyancing & Disbursements	$2,000 (estimate)
Total cash required to settle	$101,382

This that meant that the loan amount would be 90% of the property value, or $645,750. As this was an investment property, we opted for an *interest only* loan to help us optimise cash flow and prioritise our own home's mortgage.

What did the cash flow look like?

Here are the numbers in the first year, annualised.

Rental income	$34,060 ($655 per week)
Less expenses	
Interest (interest only at 2.69%)	$17,371
Agent commission	$3,185
Letting fees	$655
Council Rates	$1,800
Body corporate	$4,440
Landlord Insurance	$400
Total outlays	$27,851
Net cash flow before tax	$6,209
Tax Adjustments	
Depreciation – construction	$8,111
Depreciation – fittings & furniture	~$14,000 (estimate, as it straddled two financial years)
Total non-cash tax deductions	$22,111
Taxable Income (Taxable Loss) from property	($15,902)
Tax reduction at 39% tax rate	$6,201
Net cash after tax from property ($6,201 + $6,209)	$12,410
Net cash for after tax as a % of money invested ($12,410 divided by $101,382)	12.24%

Thanks for bearing with the numbers! What I wanted to illustrate here is the way I calculate the net cash return on a property. Now, keep in mind, this percentage return is *before* any capital growth. I don't invest in property where I need to make a capital gain from it to make it worthwhile, but capital growth is something I will definitely take, if it's there.

The rate of 12.24% is also an after-tax investment return rate. If we were to gross it up by the tax rate of 39% to see what an equivalent investment would need to earn before tax, then it would require an investment return of 20.06% before tax, to compete with this. I'm not sure many investments can produce this pre-tax rate consistently.

Gross Return vs. Return On Your Cash

I also want to illustrate the net cash return in the case that we were to *not* borrow any money from the bank, but instead pay for that property with cash only . (It's not that we had the cash to purchase that property in full, but sometimes a question that clients ask is: "Should I take out a loan if I have the cash in the bank?").

I'll let the following numbers do the talking:

Net cash flow before tax (from above)	$6,209
Add back interest expense as would not need to pay it	$17,371
Adjust for tax at 39% (I've skipped the workings in detail here, but this is the answer – the property would now make a taxable gain)	($573) expense
Net rental income after tax	$23,007
Total money invested – ($717,500 + $27,632 + $2,000)	$747,132
Net rental after tax return as a % of money invested	3.08%

I hope that illustrates the difference in return on your money if you leverage using the bank's money, versus if you were to buy it cash with your own money. Your net after-tax return rate is about four times better when leveraging the bank's money. This also keeps some of your capital (cash) free to invest in additional properties or other investments, which in turn diversifies your portfolio.

Buying The Property Through SMSF

In *Step 6: Long Term Wealth*, I did mention the potential of buying property in your SMSF. A high number of our clients set up SMSF's to do this and, as I shared, you can also borrow money from the bank in super. There's a lot more information in Step 6 if you want to go into it in detail, but I just wanted to mention again that it is possible to purchase a property in super. You can even receive negative gearing benefits if the property is owned in super and it is negatively geared.

In super, the capital gains tax rate (if you've sold a property for a gain) is 10% tax, if you've owned it for more than 12 months. Otherwise, it's a 15% tax rate if you've owned it for less than 12 months (or tax-free if you're in tax-free pension mode). These rates are *much less* than the outside of super-maximum capital gains tax rate of 23.5% if you've owned it for more than 12 months, or 47% tax if you've owned it for less than 12 months.

Now, the tax rate on capital gains outside of super does depend on what your marginal tax rate is, so it won't always be as high as the rates I've just mentioned (depending on your other income). But regardless, it's more than likely going to be a lot less tax if the gain is made inside of super.

Conclusion

I do wish you luck if you choose to invest in property. I've seen many of our clients earn significant amounts of money on property and, as I said earlier, every single one of our wealthiest clients has property as part of their investing strategy. I've also heard stories of people who lost money in property, which is why I strongly recommend doing enough research on the topic before you invest. Make sure that you're comfortable with whatever you choose and protect the downside or risk of capital loss as much as you can.

In the step we are concluding now, the property we *didn't* talk about was the house that you live in. In Australia, there's a fairly the strong mindset to pay off your own home mortgage as quickly as you can. In the next Step, we're going to run through an underutilised (and often unknown) strategy to help pay off your mortgage in a fraction of the time you otherwise would.

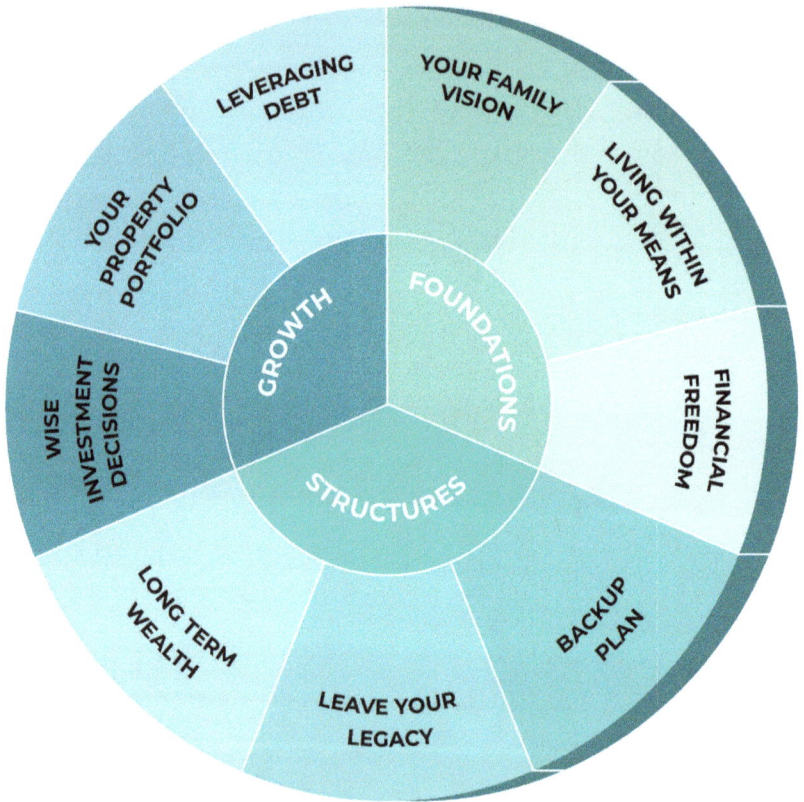

Step 9:
Leveraging Debt

We have now reached the final step of *Wealth For Life!* Here, we are going to talk about making the most of debt. This topic goes hand-in-hand with everything we've spoken about to date, especially when it comes to property investment as we covered in the previous step.

In this step, I shared two scenarios: one was leveraging debt where the after-tax return rate of an investment property was over 12%. This was compared to the second scenario where if you paid cash for that same property, the return was about 3% on the money invested. This is one example of the benefit of leveraging debt correctly.

Getting debt right can also have other benefits, especially when you use the process called **debt recycling** to increase the speed at which your own home's mortgage is paid off.

Then, once you have cleared your mortgage, you own an income-producing asset, as well as your own home, with zero non-tax-deductible debt.

Is Debt A Dirty Word?

When I was growing up, I noticed that my parents did whatever they could to clear the mortgage on their own home. The focus was to get rid of debt because debt was a dirty word and had negative connotations. I can understand this, as having no mortgage on your own home secures your house and, unless you fail to pay council rates, there are not many ways that you are going to become homeless. I also agree that debt can definitely be a trap for people if they mismanage it, or if they go too far into debt without having proper strategies to manage it.

This being the case, I feel like using debt in a productive way to turbocharge your ability to invest is actually a great thing. It brings forward your ability to purchase large assets, like property, by leveraging the bank's money instead of having to save longer to be able to pay cash for a property.

You will also ride the increase in market value between when you can loan money for the property versus when you're finally ready to pay cash for it. This in itself can offset any interest or other expenses associated with borrowing, and more!

Being able to understand and manage debt will truly make a difference in your long-term wealth creation ability.

Good Debt Vs. Bad Debt

It is important to understand good debt versus bad debt.

I've heard two ways the phrase "Good debt vs bad debt" can be used:

1. The first is where good debt is associated with an asset and bad debt includes debt associated with personal expenses, such as paying a credit card off or a taking out a personal loan for living expenses.

2. The second way I've heard this term used is where good debt is related to an income-producing asset such as property, shares, or a business and bad debt is associated with non-tax-deductible debt, such as personal credit card debt, personal loans, or even the mortgage on your own home.

From my perspective, I see debt relating to income-producing assets as very productive, as it is used to purchase an investment asset and is tax deductible for the interest that you pay. This works as long as the income from the asset is quality and secure.

'OK debt' in my books, would be debt associated with an asset but that is not necessarily tax deductible. This would include your own home, and I struggled to consider this bad debt because you are paying off an asset that, if you do make a capital gain on it, will be tax-free.

Debt on your own home often has a lower interest rate than tax-deductible debt as well, and we've seen people's lifestyles changed completely when they have made gains on their main residence in a rising property market. An example of this would be bringing retirement forward when a couple makes an unexpected gain on their own home and then downsized (or 'right sized') to something more appropriate for their retirement. They do this with a lot more tax-free money in their bank account than they thought they would have. So, if the debt on your house has helped you get into something like that strong asset position, then, again, I would struggle to call that bad debt.

'Bad debt' to me is high interest, a non-tax-deductible debt. A simple example of this is a credit card that's been racked up for living expenses, or unsecured bank loans sourced to pay for holidays or weddings. You can pay a huge amount of interest on the debt that has no underlying asset. It's also not tax deductible. So, this would be my first priority of debt that I would recommend people get rid of. Then, I would turn my attention to the 'OK debt' of clearing my own home mortgage.

Finally, if I had the urge to clear more debt after the family home is paid off, the only debt left would be good debt, AKA investment-related and tax-deductible debt.

Other Debt Lingo

There is a fair bit of lingo that goes along with loaning money from banks and when working with mortgage brokers to get a good outcome for you and your family. The purpose of this section is to run through some things that you may run into when you are dealing with banks and mortgage brokers.

I'm not a mortgage broker now, but I did do the study required for it and held my registration for a few years so I would understand the industry. However, please know that this is not for credit advice. It is just general information about the terminology.

Fixed VS Variable Rate

A **fixed interest rate** is one that is fixed usually for a certain amount of time from when the loan is taken out.

Usually, you can lock in a fixed rate for say 1, 2, 3, 4 or 5 years, but the time does differ from bank to bank. The benefits of a fixed rate are a certainty, that your loan repayments won't change in the time frame during which your interest rate is fixed.

This can be good in a market where rates are likely to increase. But, in a market where rates are decreasing, you won't get the benefit of reduced repayments when the rate is dropping.

In comparison, a variable rate will vary as the Reserve Bank of Australia (RBA) adjusts the interest rate from time to time. At the time of writing, for the past decade or so, the cash rate had consistently dropped right down to a low of 0.1% in the more recent years (as an emergency reaction during COVID).

Over this time, variable rates have been reducing. After a few years of record low cash rates, they consistently increased in order to combat inflation. The result of these increases was a volatile reaction from consumer confidence, the media going nuts as usual, and variable rate mortgage repayments increasing.

Note: if you have a 'fixed rate' mortgage where the fixed rate is coming to an end, your loan will likely revert to the current 'variable' rate for that bank.

Principal and Interest VS Interest Only

When it comes to repayment options, you've got another decision to make: will you pay Interest only or Principal and Interest repayments?

Interest only is similar to a fixed rate loan. There is a time limit on how long the interest-only repayment term goes for, then the loan will revert to **principal and interest.** Each month, you are only paying the interest component, instead of any of the original loan amount reducing. This means that the repayments will be less than a principal and interest loan, but it won't be reduced.

From a tax perspective, interest only is more appropriate for an investment property compared to if you have a mortgage on the home you live in still. Why? Because, from a tax perspective, you will be better off focusing on clearing the non-tax-deductible debt first.

Principal and interest repayments are where you pay the interest plus a portion of the original loan amount each month. This method is likely to reduce the overall interest that you pay over the loan term, as you will be paying slightly less interest each month, as the total loan outstanding will be reduced in value.

Offset Account

An **offset account** is an account that your lender sets up. If you put money into this account, then it offsets an amount of interest against the loan it is 'linked' to.

Most offset accounts are 100% offset. This means that for every dollar you put into the account, it will act is if a dollar of the loan was 'repaid' for the purpose of calculating the interest. That means if you had a loan of $100,000, and a 100% offset account with $100,000 in it, you would pay $0 in interest. Be careful though, as some banks don't offer 100% offsets on certain products.

Offset accounts are great to put extra savings into to offset the interest, especially non-tax-deductible interest on your own home.

LVR

LVR is an acronym for **Loan to Value Ratio**. It is expressed as a percent, that your loan is to the security (or property) it is attached to.

Here is a simple example of this. Let's say you have a property worth $1,000,000, with a loan attached to this of $800,000. The Loan to Value Ratio would be 80%. Banks like to keep the LVR under 80% if they can as it is less risk to the bank – otherwise, you are usually required to pay 'LMI' (see next definition).

LMI

LMI is an acronym for **Lenders Mortgage Insurance**. This is an insurance that the bank is required to take out in certain circumstances. The most common is that your LVR exceeds 80%.

The bank needs to get insurance to cover your loan in case you are not able to pay it. The bank passes this insurance cost onto you and they can capitalise it into your loan. For example, let's say you have a loan that will be an LVR of 90%. The bank may offer you a loan where they add the LMI into your loan, although you also would have the option to pay it on the settlement of the bank issuing you that loan.

There are certain industries, such as certain medical and professional services, where banks waive this requirement up to say 90%, but it does depend bank to bank. In this case, the bank is essentially self-insuring your loan, as they believe that people working in those professions are less likely to default on their loans.

How To Pay Off Your Home In A Quarter Of The Time

While I had heard of this concept before, it was only around 2018 where I fully understood the power of **debt recycling.**

The process is where you use the equity in your own home to purchase income-producing assets, such as an investment property. This increases your tax-deductible debt but also provides you with an income stream and tax benefits that you can use to pay off your own home loan in addition to your existing income.

The goal of debt recycling is to clear your own home's non-tax-deductible mortgage much quicker compared to if you were to not implement the debt recycling strategy.

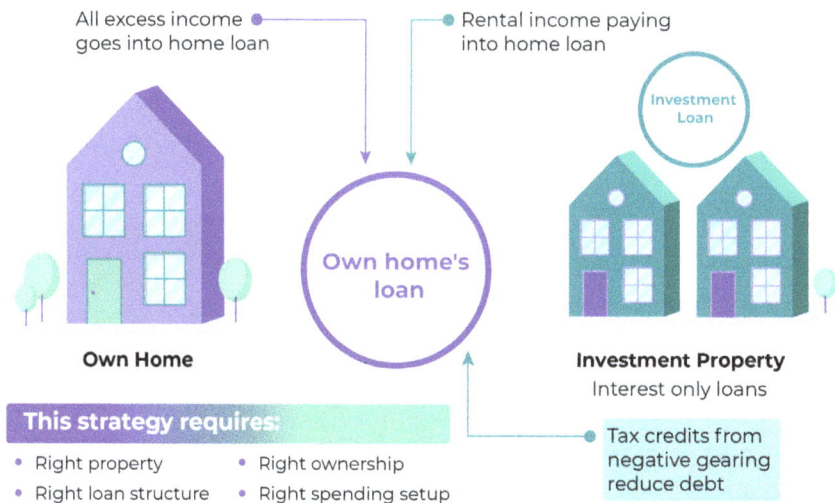

All excess income goes into home loan

Rental income paying into home loan

Investment Loan

Own home's loan

Own Home

Investment Property
Interest only loans

This strategy requires:
- Right property
- Right loan structure
- Right ownership
- Right spending setup

Tax credits from negative gearing reduce debt

This does not mean that when your home loan is cleared that you will have no debt. Rather, it means that any debt you have remaining is associated with an income-producing asset and is tax deductible. It will likely also be paying for itself.

In order to work well, this strategy needs the right investment property, the right loan structure, the right ownership of the investment property, and the right personal spending set-up. Let's explore these in detail now.

The Right Property

Cash flow is the focus in terms of the **right property**. We look for properties with a good rental return, tenant appeal (to minimise and hopefully avoid untenanted time) and good tax depreciation. This often means that we will purchase a newly constructed property, rather than an existing property where we miss out on that second layer of depreciation. A new property also helps to reduce maintenance and repair costs compared to an older property, which may require far more frequent repairs, maintenance, and ongoing upkeep.

The Right Loan Structure

There are a few guidelines for your loan structure that helps focus on clearing your home's mortgage:

- You have an offset account with your mortgage where you can park any excess funds. This offsets your non-tax-deductible interest

- The mortgage on your investment property is interest only, at least until your own home loan is paid off

- You have a loan on your own home that you can make additional repayments on, without penalty

The Right Ownership

Whose name an investment property is purchased in, will determine who pays the tax – or who gets the tax credit – in the event that the property is negatively geared. If a client and their spouse are both employees, we will often look to purchase the property in the name of the highest salary person, who would normally be in the highest tax bracket of the two. This person will then get the biggest tax credit if the property is negatively geared.

If we are dealing with clients that are self-employed who use company or trust structures to run their businesses through, then we have the ability to purchase the property either in their own names or in a trust. This assumes that we can transfer the profit from the business into that trust to offset any negative gearing.

The Right Spending Set-Up

There are a couple of things to keep in mind to get the right spending set up.

The first one is to make sure that when you purchase the investment property, that you borrow as much of that property as you can using the equity in your house for the deposit (ordinarily the 20% plus stamp duty). The remaining 80% that you need to borrow from the bank can be secured against the investment property itself.

That covers the purchase itself, but what about the ongoing costs?

If you have the ability to have a separate loan account on your mortgage that you can allocate for all of the rental expenses, then you can pay your ongoing investment property expenses from a new loan account. Then, you can send the gross rent from your property straight into your home offset account. This will maximise your overall tax-deductible interest and pay off your own home's loan quicker.

An Example Of Debt Recycling In Action

SCENARIO 1:
Pay down mortgage

SCENARIO 2:
Pay down mortgage leveraging other properties

Repayment timeline: 30 years

Repayment timeline: 8.4 years

Option One, is where a $500,000 mortgage is paid off over 30 years.

This was our reality when we purchased a home for the first time. We were only paying the minimum payments on our home loan. I remember that the repayments were around $22,000 per year (our loan amount was $420,000, though).

Now, let's say that you combine your minimum repayments with the property example I gave in *Step 8* of our investment property, the apartment in Windsor. This provided an additional $12,000 per year (approximately) in after-tax money that we could then put into our home loan. This increased the annual payments on the property by around 54.5%, compared to what we were doing by meeting the minimum repayments only.

The result was that instead of repaying our home loan in 30 years, through the purchase of two investment properties, we would be on track to clear our own home's mortgage in 8.4 years. At the end of the 8.4 years, we would be left with two investment properties that still had loans on them, producing tax-effective income for us.

When we first learned of this strategy, we then went to purchase our first investment property. We had secured it before the market rose in recent years. So, not only did this strategy work very well from a debt recycling perspective, but it also raised our net asset position through the capital growth in the properties.

Closing Comments On Leveraging Debt: Work With A Broker

My strong recommendation is to work with a good mortgage broker to get you the best outcome when it comes to your property loans. Also, if you do own a business, make sure that you find someone who is fairly experienced with self-employed people. We only work with self-employed clients, so we have found a broker that matches the unique requirements of our clients. Please reach out to us if you would like an introduction.

Brokers have access to multiple banks. They also have access to software that compares the offers from different banks against your personal requirements in seconds. This beats you going to 10 banks, pitching your position to them, and hoping that they will show you their best deal!

They also do a lot of the heavy lifting with the banks, too. There is a lot they do behind the scenes that you don't even see. So, be sure to work with a good one, and keep checking in with them every few years, or as your requirements change.

Part Summary

I hope that the last three steps talking about **growth** have been a nice icing on the cake of getting the foundations and the structures right when it comes to building wealth for life.

As a reminder, it is very rare that wealth creation is a quick or overnight process. So, make sure that you choose your strategy well, and commit to it for years.

If you feel out of your depth, please reach out for professional help with whatever you are looking to achieve. If we can't help you directly, because we're not licenced to do so or aren't the best people to help you, then we can put you in touch with who you need to help you achieve your goals.

Implementation Checklist

Step 7	
Have you reviewed your current investment strategy?	☐
Have you sought out advice where you feel stuck or need help investing?	☐
Step 8	
Have you read the tax benefits of properties and made the most of them with your current properties?	☐
Have you run the numbers to see your ROI on any existing properties you have?	☐
Step 9	
Have you reviewed your loans with a mortgage broker in the last two years?	☐
Have you sought out advice to see if a debt recycling strategy might be beneficial for your family?	☐

Conclusion

I hope you've enjoyed reading this book as much as I have enjoyed developing it over the past few years as I've presented the *Wealth For Life* workshop to clients, along with experiencing my own wealth creation journey.

I do want to remind and encourage you that if you feel like your goals or the targets are well out of reach, to just **believe** they are possible. Why? Because you will likely underestimate what you can achieve in five to ten years. I know I definitely did. Where it will fall over, though, is if you have read this book and gained knowledge around wealth creation... but then you don't do anything or don't do much as a result.

Make a concentrated effort to get a plan in place. A business coach I know and have worked with over the years says that every business owner runs *two* businesses. The first business is their profession or what they went into business for. The second is the careful management of their business profits to invest them and create additional wealth for themselves and their family.

Consider the effort that you put into your first business. I don't necessarily think that both creations should be a full-time job, but your wealth creation strategy does deserve a decent amount of planning up front and then ongoing attention to make sure that you are on track and always heading in a better direction.

The other thing that makes the difference between a stressful, good, or great wealth creation journey is having the right team in place. I'm not telling you that Inspire or I have the answer to everything, and, in terms of the right team, I definitely am not referring only to having a good accountant.

It also means having a good lawyer, insurance specialist (for both general insurance and life insurances), mortgage broker, financial planner, property advisers, property managers, and other aspirational friends or contacts who are on the wealth creation journey. These people have been key in my own wealth creation journey. They can help take advantage of great opportunities and protect you from costly mistakes or downsides.

I would also love to hear any feedback you have about the book and the changes you've made as a result of the ideas and suggestions shared. Please feel free to connect with me on social media! My handle on Facebook, Instagram, and LinkedIn is 'benwalkerca'.

If you'd like to learn more about these wealth creation topics (and many others), please read Inspires newsletter. You can subscribe on our website http://inspire. accountants. We hold many workshops and webinars on different topics, and the lens we look through is the lens of business owners.

So, from here on, please enjoy implementing these strategies and sharing them with your spouse to bring them along for the journey. I truly believe that the better we can make our own lives, the better we are then positioned to help those around us including our family or friends, our communities, or even on a global scale.

Do you want to learn more about my accounting firm, Inspire?

Thanks again for reading my book, and hope you enjoyed it.

If you'd like to explore more about my accounting firm Inspire – Life Changing Accountants, please head to our website at https://inspire.accountants/

Got a problem with Tax, Your Accountant or Business Structures? The solution is a rapid fire Q & A session with an Inspire Accountant.

Book a phone call or a zoom chat with one of accountants, by heading to https://inspire.accountants/chat - or you can use the QR Code below.

The most common problems people reach out for are:

- A feeling that you might be paying too much tax
- Wanting to Change Accountants
- Needing to set up a NEW business structure
- Understanding your existing structure
- Considering the move to Xero
- Getting up to date with your TAX
- That the ATO is on your back
- Pulling more cash out of your business
- Finding ways to boost your profits
- Not knowing your numbers

Acknowledgements

I want to acknowledge and send my gratitude to:

- My loving wife who has been there with me through the good and the bad, the broke and the doing okay times. Thank you for the support and creating this beautiful thing called life and family together with me... Love you!

- My parents, Trish & Jeff, for being a great example at working seriously hard to provide for your family. You gave me so many opportunities growing up and supported me with getting Inspire off the ground (at the detriment of accelerating the growth of your grey hairs!).

- My grandfather, who passed away a few years ago, for his inspiration of being able to step back from business to take care of my grandmother when she got cancer. That was an eye opener to me of how creating a business can give you options in life and allow you to put your family first.

- The awesome team at Inspire. Without you, the vision for Inspire would still be a dream. Now, we're living it.

- The hundreds of clients I've worked with from the start of Inspire where I have seen your journey growing your own business, wealth, and families.

- To all the partners of Inspire who help to implement the strategies I mention in this book. Thanks for doing what you do to provide great outcomes for our clients.

- To you, reading this book: thank you for giving up a few hours of your life to read my philosophies. I hope it was a worthwhile investment and remember: The Power of Any Idea is only in its implementation (Thanks to my mentor Paul Dunn, for that one!).

About The Author

Ben Walker founded *Inspire – Life Changing Accountants* at the age of 23 with nothing but a borrowed printer, a laptop, and a simple idea. What if, instead of just doing tax and reporting on history, accountants could give game-changing advice that could help people create a better future for their business and their family?

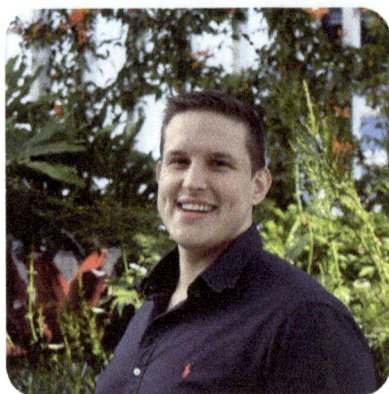

Years on, *Inspire* has been showcased as a global example of what an accounting firm should be. This is thanks to Ben's disruptive approach to throwing out timesheets and charging by the hour, his challenge of the traditional 'old school' model of the accounting industry, and his belief that accountants change lives: their own lives, their team's, their clients, and others around the world.

Ben is a winner of the coveted *Anthill Online 30under30 Award*, was named a finalist in the *Brisbane Young Entrepreneur of the Year, Australian Accounting Award's Mentor of the Year, Boutique Firm of the Year* and *Marketing Program Of The Year* for 2022. He has been featured in many publications including the *Courier Mail, Dent*

Podcast with Glen Carlson, *Small Business Big Marketing Podcast* with Tim Reid, *Brisbane Business News & B Mag*.

Ben has also been a Chartered Accountant for more than a decade, and is the Author of multiple books. Today, while he continues to lead Inspire as Chartered Accountant & Founder, Ben's goal is to inspire others create a business that gives them the freedom to put family first and make a positive difference in the world.

TO BOOK BEN FOR A SPEAKING ENGAGEMENT, FIND
OUT MORE AT
benwalker.com

TO EXPLORE WORKING WITH INSPIRE VISIT
inspire.accountants

Other Books By Ben

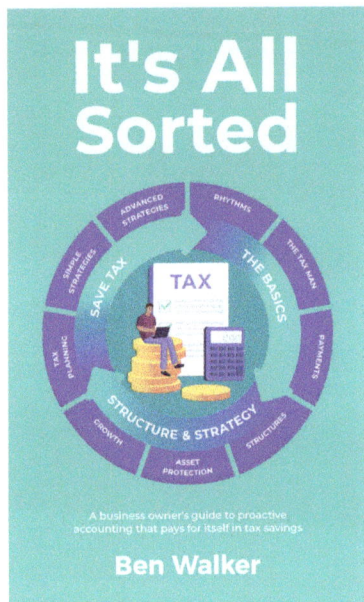

It's All Sorted

A business owner's guide to proactive accounting that pays for itself in tax savings.

In this book, we share three key ideas through our 9 Step Method:

- How to get your tax rhythms in sync, working with a proactive accountant

- Structures and the strategy you need to understand to grow your business through the various stages

- The key strategies of how we've saved literally tens of millions of dollars for our clients in tax savings

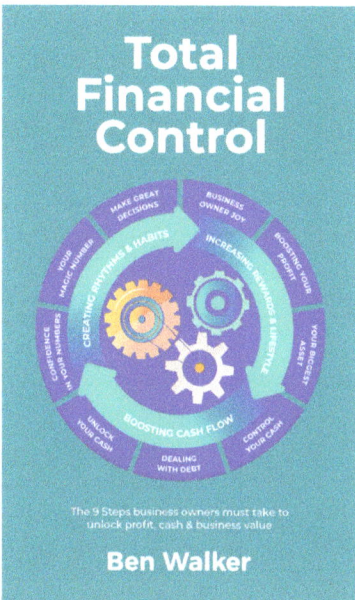

Total Financial Control

The 9 Steps business owners must take to unlock profit, cash & business value.

In this book, we share three key ideas through our 9 Step Method:

- Understanding what drives you and how that feeds your growth of profit and business value

- Boosting your cash flow to make it work for you and using debt to your advantage

- Building in the rhythms and habits required to create a high level of financial performance